It Shall Be Given

God Bless ya brother,

I pray this book & the songs bless you & your family!

— Chris

It Shall Be Given

Christopher Maskey

Copyright © 2017 by Christopher Maskey.

Library of Congress Control Number: 2017907886
ISBN: Hardcover 978-1-5434-2418-8
Softcover 978-1-5434-2417-1
eBook 978-1-5434-2416-4

All rights reserved. No part of this book may be reproduced or transmitted in any form or by any means, electronic or mechanical, including photocopying, recording, or by any information storage and retrieval system, without permission in writing from the copyright owner.

Scripture quotations marked KJV are from the Holy Bible, King James Version (Authorized Version). First published in 1611. Quoted from the KJV Classic Reference Bible, Copyright © 1983 by The Zondervan Corporation.

Any people depicted in stock imagery provided by Thinkstock are models, and such images are being used for illustrative purposes only.
Certain stock imagery © Thinkstock.

Print information available on the last page.

Rev. date: 05/17/2017

To order additional copies of this book, contact:
Xlibris
1-888-795-4274
www.Xlibris.com
Orders@Xlibris.com
760955

Contents

Opening Prayer..vii
Introduction..ix

Chapter 1   December 10, 1982..........................1
Chapter 2   The Early Years................................9
Chapter 3   Setting an Example..........................19
Chapter 4   St. Mary's..25
Chapter 5   A Boy into a Man.............................31
Chapter 6   Blinking Eyes...................................39
Chapter 7   The Altar Boy..................................47
Chapter 8   That One Summer...........................59
Chapter 9   The New Kid....................................67
Chapter 10 The News..75
Chapter 11 Remission...89
Chapter 12 The New Me.....................................95
Chapter 13 The Battle.......................................117
Chapter 14 Getting Tired.................................135
Chapter 15 Born Again....................................149
Chapter 16 Closing Thoughts..........................161

Opening Prayer

Heavenly Father,

    I ask You, Lord, please fill me with the right words and thoughts to use as I go along and attempt to write this book. I pray that You allow me to help others who read it by sharing my story in a way that is pleasing to You in hopes that they will accept Your Son, Jesus Christ, as their personal Lord and Savior. I give You all the praise and glory and recognize that it is not me who is speaking through these memories but the presence of the Holy Spirit that is working through me and guiding me in each and every page of this book. I thank You, Heavenly Father, for all You have done and continue to do in my life, and it is You to whom I give all the glory. In these last days before the imminent rapture, I ask that You save as many souls, Lord, who read this book by showing them the things You have already shown me. Please, Lord, let this book give sight to those who presently do not know You as their personal Savior and shed light on those who are spiritually blind and sit in darkness in this present world. I ask this all in the great name of Jesus Christ, amen.

Introduction

The introduction to every successful motivational book is supposed to do three key things, or so I am told: (1) establish the reasoning behind writing the book, (2) define the direct audience you are looking to attract in the book, and (3) showcase the benefits the reader will experience when reading the book. So apparently, this is the time where I am supposed to strategically think of some clever words to use and hope that after reading them, you will be so drawn to this book that you will absolutely have no choice but to continue to move to the first chapter and absorb what I am trying to give you. With that being said, allow me to take care of those three steps by plainly saying this. The reason behind me writing this book is because I want to help you *save your soul*. That's it.

Establish the reasoning behind the book? The reason is because I want all of you to be *saved*. The only way to be saved is for you to accept Jesus Christ as your Lord and Savior and allow Him to wash your sins away with His blood that He willingly shed on the cross for the entirety of the human race.

Define the direct audience? *You*, as in anyone who has eyes to see or ears to hear. Everyone is invited into the kingdom of God, those who allow God to speak to them through His Word (the Bible).

Finally, showcase the benefits the reader will experience? What could be more beneficial to someone than for them to gain their *soul?* The Bible says, "What shall it profit a man if he shall gain the world and lose his own soul?" Material things have no value compared to your salvation and where you will be going after this earthly life is over. This book will encourage you and lead you to Jesus Christ, and He will *save your soul*, nothing more and nothing less. We have a choice to either spend eternity in heaven with Jesus or spend eternity in torment, burning in the fire of hell forever. That is what is at stake.

The short span of time we have here on earth is like a blink of an eye compared to eternity. Try and picture forever; you cannot do it. Our human minds cannot put together a conscious thought or image that will accurately describe what forever will be like. Sadly, the majority of the people who have lived and died on this planet are burning in hell as I write this because they have not accepted Jesus Christ as Lord and Savior, but this same fate does not have to be for you and me. If you are a believer already, that is great; this book will bless your heart and hopefully reassure you as you continue on this narrow path of life that we need to remain on. If you are a nonbeliever and have your doubts, then I just ask you to please take the time and continue reading this book and allow the Holy Spirit to work inside of you as you read along.

Now the next thing we need to discuss is how exactly can reading this book help you to allow Jesus Christ to save your soul? The Bible is the only place that you should go for God-given truth because it is His Word. When seeking God in your life, I encourage all of you to do your homework and not just take what I say in this book to be true but to go to the scriptures and read the Word of God for yourself.

With that being said, the best way I can help others come to the Lord is by showing you what I have gone through in my life and how God has helped me to overcome much. Nothing I have done on my own has brought me to where I am in life; it was all by the grace of God that I am still alive and well today. He has had a plan for me even before I was born, just as He does for all of you reading this. Many of you are experiencing all sorts of troubles and pain in your lives. I once heard Pastor Torrance Nash say one night while he was preaching, "The greater the calling, the greater the test." My life is a testament of faith that I want to use to help others dedicate their lives to the Lord in these last days. The Bible says in John 3:17, "For God did not send His Son into the world to condemn the world, but in order that the world might be saved through Him." The single most important thing we can do with our lives is finding Jesus Christ, and I hope my story can lead you in the right direction toward Him.

Chapter 1

December 10, 1982

My mother always used to tell me how all she ever wanted in life was to be a mom. She told me a story one time about how she and my father were having difficulty getting pregnant, so she placed a note into her Bible saying, "Lord, if it's your will, please let me have a child."

Years later, she was feeling really sick one day, so she went to the doctor's office to see what was causing it. The doctor came out and told her that she was indeed pregnant. She could not wait to go home and tell my dad. When she got home, she decided to read her Bible like she normally did, and what do ya know, that same note that she wrote years before about wanting a child popped out and landed on the floor. She opened up the note and immediately started crying, knowing that God had finally answered her prayers, and she was going to be a mom!

Before I get into the story of my life, I think it is important to let you know all about my mother and my father. My mother was literally everything that a child could ask for in a parent. She was loving, patient, funny, nurturing, and really just the kindest person I have ever met in my entire life. She was the oldest of four children. She grew up taking care of my three uncles way before I was born. I really believe her main purpose in life was to help others, and it just so happens that I was fortunate enough to call this beloved person my mother. My mother was beautiful; she had long straight dark hair that looked almost black and beautiful kind brown eyes that would light up every time she smiled. She was always smiling. My mother was just always a happy person with a genuine smile, not like one of those fake smiles that people give you when they really do not like you but they feel they have to. She had one of those smiles that would draw you into her happiness and make you forget about anything negative.

Now onto my dad. My dad was . . . well, how can I put this, let's just say he was different from my mother. I will try to describe him from what I have been told and from what I have seen in pictures due to the fact that I really didn't know him that well. My dad's full name was Christopher James Maskey, but everyone called him CJ. He was the kind of person you would want to be around come Friday afternoon and you were looking for a party. In my understanding, he had tons of friends and was always the one who could make you laugh if you were having a rough day. He seemed like a good guy, just not exactly the model idea of someone who needed to be responsible for the life of a child very shortly.

My mom and dad were dating for a long period of time but were never officially married. I remember my mom telling me how excited he was when she first told him that she was pregnant and they were having a child. I would later find out that his excessive partying left her alone for most of the nine months of her pregnancy with me. I am sure he was there for support but not to the extent that a woman really needed when going through something as emotional and difficult as getting ready for her first baby, or any baby for that matter.

December 10, 1982—ready or not, world, here I come! I was born in Poughkeepsie, New York, at a local hospital on a cold winter night full of snow. Okay, I am lying; I have no idea what the weather was like that day, but it sure sounds better, doesn't it? So yeah, it was a cold snow-filled evening, and I was finally in the arms of my mother. I really have no idea whether or not my father was present for my birth. His name was on my birth certificate, so I am guessing he was there at some point. It read, Father: *Christopher J. Maskey*, which was located right on top of my name that he emphatically told my mom that he wanted my name to be Christopher James Maskey 2nd.

I only have a couple of baby pictures of myself to date. My mom and dad were there in all of them. I still have the one picture of the three of us at my baptism, and if a picture could speak a thousand words, they would have all been good ones. They looked like a happy couple—new baby, new lives on the way—but underneath, things were not always as they seemed.

My mother was content with just being a mom, focusing all her time and energy on to me. From what I had been told, my father could not escape the party life and had trouble battling alcohol and drug addiction. One day my mother said enough was enough and finally decided to kick him out.

We were living in a small house in a town called Cold Spring in Upstate New York. My mother loved visiting Cold Spring way before she decided to move there. The town had been known for its antique shops and its great views of the Hudson River. People from all over would come just to walk around and take pictures, and it's still like that even today. It's the type of town where everybody knows everybody, but still, it was quiet enough for her to start a new life. It was the perfect place to raise a child since you were more likely to get hit by a meteor than be a victim of a crime happening to you inside of this quiet little town.

My dad had moved back to where he was originally born and raised in the city of Newburgh, New York—a city that was, at the time (and still is), known for its extreme drug problems and constant violence. I know what you're thinking. It's probably not the most ideal place for someone who is already battling a drug problem to move to. And you're 100 percent right, but nonetheless, he decided that was where he was going to live.

During the time that they were broken up, my mother had met a man at IBM where they both worked for years. He seemed to have had all the qualities that she was looking for in a man that my father just did not have. He was an air force veteran who had previously been stationed in England for some years but was now back in America and working at IBM like my mother. His name was Doug, and he would end up being the most influential man in my entire life. He was responsible, loving, and always there for my mom whenever she needed him.

Being a full-time working single mother, she found it tough, I am sure, but she could always rely on Doug to come and help her whenever she needed it. A big part of my mother's life was her love for God, and it was perfect for her to find someone like Doug, who also had the same admiration for the Lord.

They continued dating throughout the first couple of years of my life, and things were great. Though my father was living in Newburgh, he would still come by from time to time to see me, but at that age, I really do not remember any of it. I am sure, for him, it must have been tough to see another man around his child and the woman whom he had loved, but he never did anything to change his lifestyle so he could be a part of our lives.

As time went on, my mother and Doug finally decided to get married. I was around four years old when the two of them tied the knot, and I could not have been happier. I was now getting a stepfather, and Doug was officially going to step in and take care of his new stepson. I know I never really looked at him as a stepfather though. To me, he was the only thing I had ever known as far as being a father figure. CJ was my dad, but Doug was indeed my father.

I do not remember much of their wedding, but I do recall that it was small and only a handful of people were there to celebrate. I remember how my mother came over to me and kissed me on my cheek and just sat there smiling at me, almost as if to say "I'm finally happy." She was happy that she was married to the man that she loved and happy that her only son was not going to grow up in this world without a positive role model in his life.

Chapter 2

The Early Years

My mother's side of the family was small, but we were all extremely close growing up. Traditionally, we would all get together on Sundays to hang out and have dinner at my grandparents' house. My grandmother was literally one of the greatest cooks alive, and my grandfather, well, he was a man of few words. Most days he would be upstairs alone in the bedroom, occupying himself with *The Three Stooges* videocassettes that he would usually have on replay. It was well known that my grandfather's main hobby of choice was his fishing. If he had it his way, he would be on the side of a river with a pole and container of bait sitting right next to him all day, every day.

I remember when my grandparents would babysit me, my grandfather would always take me on the front porch, and we would count how many cars would pass by before my mother came to pick me up. Usually, I would get a kick out of him pointing out the big trucks, but nothing excited me more than when I saw my mother's blue van pull into the driveway. My grandfather would not open up to too many people, but it seemed like he and I had a pretty unique relationship.

One Christmas, when I was little, we were all downstairs as a family, opening gifts, and my grandfather was upstairs alone, relaxing on his bed. I took it upon myself to grab all his presents and run upstairs so he wasn't alone and had someone to open gifts with. I kicked the door open like any four-year-old kid would and ran over to him. He laughed and asked "what are you doing up here, pal?" while shaking his head. I was too small to jump on the bed, so he grabbed me and plopped me down next to him. Of course, playing on the television was his all-time favorite holiday movie, *A Christmas Carol* starring the one and only Alastair Simms.

My mother would come up the stairs a couple minutes later to find me and my grandpop lying back on the bed watching the movie together. She would always point out what a big heart I had to take time away from playing with toys to go be with my grandfather so he wasn't alone on Christmas. I really enjoyed spending time with my grandfather. Plus it helped that he always shared his Hershey's Kisses with me when I would go up for visits.

As I said before, my grandmother was the chef of the family, and her Sunday afternoon meatball wedges are something that I will never forget. The smell of the sauce cooking when I would first walk into the house was incredible! The perfect blend of roasted garlic and tomatoes infused with mouthwatering tender pork chops. I used to love just being in the kitchen, watching her slice up the garlic so thin it melted like butter as soon as it joined the other ingredients in the pot.

Besides cooking the best food around, my grandmother was a simple woman. As long as she had her books, cigarettes, and a nice comfortable couch to read on, she was content. She spent her whole life working in the cafeteria of a local school, and she was the first person I've ever known that went her whole life without ever learning how to drive. When I would ask her why she never wanted to drive, she would laugh and say, "I'm close to everything I need. Why would I want to drive?" She was, without a doubt, the backbone of our family, and we all loved her dearly.

Other family members that would frequent these Sunday gatherings were my uncle Tim and his son Tim that we all called Little Tim, my uncle Tom, Aunt Kathy, and my other two cousins Jamie and Jill.

My uncle Tim was the family comedian and was always looking to do something funny to get some attention. My uncle Tom was more laid-back, but when the two of them would crack on each other back and forth, often times my uncle Tom would be the victorious one. My uncle Tim, Uncle Tom, and Doug would usually be seen at the dining-room table trading baseball cards and talking about sports together. Doug got along great with everyone in the family, and for my grandfather to like you, that was saying something!

While the men of the house were talking about sports, the woman would be in the living room, watching television, usually in a cloud of cigarette smoke. My aunt Kathy would smoke here and there, but my mother and grandmother were the real ringleaders. They smoked in the morning, they smoked in the evening, they smoked in the car, they smoked while walking, and they smoked while sitting—I mean, they smoked any chance they could get! I don't remember too many days as a kid (if any) that I wasn't surrounded by secondhand smoke from those cigarettes.

While the guys talked sports and the woman enjoyed their television and cigarettes, the kids would be in the backyard, having a blast. My cousin Tim, a.k.a. Little Tim, was a couple years older than me, but we were really close back then. His mother and my uncle Tim had been divorced, so he spent a lot of time sleeping over at my grandma's house on the weekends. We got to spend a lot of time together. My cousin Jamie was around the same age as I was, and Jill was a couple years younger.

The four of us would be in that backyard, playing kickball or Wiffle ball all day, at least until one of us would hit the ball over the fence, thus ending our game. After the games were over, Little Tim and I couldn't wait to go play with our toys upstairs, in my grandparents' house.

If you were a boy growing up in the '80s, you pretty much got to play with the greatest toys that were ever made. Star Wars, G.I. Joes, Masters of the Universe,

Transformers—I mean, I could write a whole book just on my favorite childhood action figures.

Being an only child, I was spoiled rotten. I had access to pretty much any toy I wanted, whenever I wanted it! Little Tim also shared the same love for toys as I did, and because he was older, he always knew which cool new ones were on the verge of coming out. My grandfather had no idea that behind his door, we had literally turned the entire upstairs into an all-out battleground! Going to my grandparents' house was good for it had lots of food, toys, and fun, and that is exactly why I loved going there every weekend.

Sundays were the days to pig out and relax with the entire family, but on Saturdays, we were always out and about. Usually, on Saturdays, Doug would stay home and work on things around the house that needed fixing while my mother and I would head down to pick up my grandmother and go out for the day. Being as my cousin Little Tim was always sleeping over at my grandparents' on the weekends, he would always come with us on Saturdays too. We would pile into the back of my mother's blue van, equipped with our bag full of toys, while my mother and grandmother assumed the position as pilot and copilot in the front seats of the van.

Back in the '80s, things like cancer and smoking cigarettes didn't really have the same type of scare on people as those words do today. Cancer was a myth to most people, and cigarettes were just simply acceptable back then. My mother and grandmother would smoke nonstop while my cousin Tim and I would be in the back seat, inhaling it all on these Saturday adventures. Like I said, times were different back then, and it wasn't shocking to see a car full of kids in it with the parents smoking in the front seats.

Though it really didn't bother me as a kid, I can't imagine anyone getting away with that today with all the bans on smoking with kids in the car and the known dangers that cigarettes cause. Usually, if we weren't on our way to the malls or shopping at toy stores, we would be traveling from town to town looking for garage sales to stop at. My mother and grandmother would literally grab the *Penny Saver* magazine the night before and would highlight any local garage sales that would be going on that day and make sure we went to them all. My cousin

Little Tim and I didn't mind at all because we always went home with a bag full of goodies.

Tag sales, garage sales, rummage sales—you name it, we were there. My grandmother would usually look for any kind of reading material for herself, and my mom would be on the hunt for knickknacks or anything that she could decorate our house with. I remember plenty of times my mother buying something at the garage sale and having to call Doug up and ask him to drive over and pick up whatever she bought because it was too big to fit in her car and she needed his pickup truck.

I can just imagine being on a ladder on a ninety-five-degree summer day, cleaning the gutters and getting a phone call saying you have to come and pick up someone else's junk that your wife just bought an hour and a half away. He was a man of great patience, I guess, because he never turned her down and would always eventually show up to take home her new purchases at these garage sales. He would get out of his truck and start shaking his head, smiling at me the whole time; it was our little inside joke about my mom and her addiction to her garage sale treasures.

Besides being in the back seat of my mother's van searching for local garage sales, I usually spent my time playing with the neighborhood kids on the weekends. We lived on a dead-end street, which meant there was hardly any traffic, so we would have the perfect setup for Wiffle ball and kickball games. I remember there was a ton of kids to play with back then, and we would literally be outside all day until the sun went down or until one of the kids got mad and took his/her ball home.

I loved being outside playing, mainly because our house was so small. No, I mean our house was really tiny! We had a small living room, a kitchen, and two tiny bedrooms, so when anyone wanted to come over and play, I would always suggest going outside to do something. My mother would always be either on the porch, watching us play, or in the game, playing with us. She was the kind of mom that just always took an interest in everything I did, and all the neighborhood kids loved being around her.

My best friend, Justin, lived right down the street from me in an apartment complex near my house. His mother had babysat me for years while my mother and Doug had been at work, so Justin and I really had been best friends since we were babies. Being as he lived so close, he spent a lot of time at my house, playing with toys and hanging out with us. This was right around the time Nintendo had come out, and we had both developed a love for video games, spending most of our time glued to the screen, trying to get Mario to save that princess he was always trying to get. Often times, Justin would come along on these weekend garage sale hunts as well, but he didn't mind since he would always come home with a bag full of toys. My mother and Doug both really took a liking to Justin, and my mom would joke, whenever he would pop his head in the door, saying, "Look, everybody, it's my adopted son Justin."

The majority of the weekends, you could find Justin at my house from Friday afternoon through Sunday night. He was like family, and being as I was an only child, he was like the brother that I never had.

Chapter 3

Setting an Example

As far back as I can remember, my mother and Doug always tried to instill the importance of having a relationship with God in my life. My mother was a strong woman of faith, and Doug often times admitted that it was her doing that led him to get even closer to the Lord. I never remember either of them forcing anything on me to read or believe in; rather, they just set an example of how to live and who to put my faith in, and I followed suit.

One night we were all sitting around, watching a movie together like we would normally do on a Saturday night. My mother picked out the movie, which was *Jesus of Nazareth*. It is tough as child to keep your attention on anything other than cartoons and superheroes. I am sure I was not really paying much attention to the movie, but I will never forget watching the infamous Crucifixion scene when the Roman soldiers tortured Jesus, and He ultimately died. I remember my mother telling me to turn my head for any other movie that had violence in it, but for some reason, she wanted me to pay attention to this one and watch it. I looked over at my mother, and it shocked me to see how upset she was at this scene, so much so that she was even in tears watching it.

When it was over, I asked, "Mommy, why are you crying? Don't you like this movie?" And she smiled at me and then said, "Pay attention to what you just saw, Chris. He is the Son of God, and He gave his own life so that one day you and I can live forever." Now to me, the words didn't really make sense. How can someone die so I can live forever? He's the Son of God? What does God look like? Even though I couldn't fully comprehend what I had just seen and heard, it was planted in my head from that day on that Jesus was someone important, very important.

After watching the movie *Jesus of Nazareth*, I was very anxious to learn more about what exactly this Jesus guy was all about. His face had looked real familiar to me, but I couldn't quite put my finger on exactly where I'd seen it before. Then I pictured the upstairs floor of my grandparents' house and how they had framed pictures of Jesus on most of the walls, and I put two and two together. So in my head, I'm thinking, *This guy must be real important to have his pictures all over the walls, and movies were made about him.*"

I was always very fascinated as a child with anything that had to do with Jesus, and I was advanced in regards to what I knew about him compared to any of the other kids that I grew up with. I was four years old when I started attending different meetings and churches, listening to people preach the Word of God. My mother and Doug knew how important it was for me, at a young age, to get acquainted with the Bible but also find a happy medium where I could still be a kid and not force anything on me.

One weekend my dad CJ had called the house and asked my mother if we could get together so he could spend some time with me. I had not seen him for a while prior to this phone call, so I recall being a little excited to hear the news that my dad wanted to finally see me.

I walked into the room where Doug was getting dressed for church and said, "Hey, you're never gonna guess what I'm doing today!"

Doug looked at me and said, "I have no idea, pal, what you got planned."

I said, "I'm going to see my dad today, and he's gonna take me to get a toy."

It's funny because I really don't remember much of that whole visit with my dad that day, but I will never forget Doug's reaction to me telling him about it. Doug patted me on the head and said, "Wow, that's great, pal. I hope you guys have a great time!"

Looking back now, I realize what a classy guy Doug was and how much he really loved me. For him to know all the problems that my father was going through and never once had a bad word to say to me about him because he knew it would break my heart as it would any child at that age was commendable. He could have easily talked down on my dad and all the problems he had, but instead, he patted me on the head and went along with my excitement for seeing him.

After the visit with my dad, I remember being anxious to come home and show Doug my new toy, which happened to be a pair of army-fatigue walkie-talkies that I had always been talking about. He seemed to be just as excited as I was to show him what I had gotten and would take the time out of whatever he was doing to sit down and play army men with me. These are the little things that he would do that probably would not seem that special for any other kid, but to me, they always stood out in my mind.

Chapter 4

St. Mary's

When I had turned five, my mother and Doug had a tough decision to make as to where to send me to school to start kindergarten. All my neighborhood friends were all going to the local public school in Cold Spring by the name of Haldane. I, of course, wanted to go where my friends would be, but my mother and Doug knew the importance of me continuing to learn about the Lord and decided to send me to a Catholic school by the name of St. Mary's. Obviously, the public school would have been the cheaper of the two options, but they both made sacrifices to make sure that I would be studying God as well as all the other subjects in school. St. Mary's was not in Cold Spring either; it was around twenty minutes away from my home in a town called Fishkill. I was not too excited about not being able to be with my friends at school, but the thought of just going to school for the first time was exciting to me.

I will never forget the first day when my Catholic school uniforms arrived in the mail, and my mother showed me what I would be wearing for the next seven years of my life. No more Nike shirts and sneakers like the rest of my friends would be wearing every day. I was going to be in a shirt and tie and dress pants from now on. Picture my mom and Doug trying to convince me that a dress shirt and tie looked really cool on me—not an easy thing to do, I know. We went out and shopped for dress shoes for me but not at Foot Locker and not at Champs Sporting Goods. Nope, I was off to the good ole shoe store where any five-year-old boy dreaded going to, I'm sure.

"Look, Chris, this one you can even put a penny in the front of the loafer, isn't that cool?" Nice try, Mom, but unfortunately, I didn't take the bait. I picked out the first pair of regular black shoes, and we got out of there as quick as possible.

I remember my first day of school like it was yesterday, believe it or not. We pulled up into the St. Mary's parking lot where, on the first day of school, all the children were lined up in a row, separated by classrooms. All the kindergarten children were lined up in the very first row, with their mothers and fathers standing on the side of each child. My mother and I got out of the car and slowly walked over to the other children. My dress shirt and tie blended in perfectly with the one hundred other kids wearing the same exact outfit. My mother was a wreck from the moment we got out of the car. She was crying like a baby at the thought of her only child finally going to kindergarten. I gave her some slack that day because there were plenty of other kids' parents who were doing the same thing, so I did not mind the excessive hugs and kisses that I was receiving.

All of a sudden, a woman walked over to my mother and me with a sticker that she put on my jacket, which had my name on it. She said, "Hello, Christopher, I am Mrs. Hernandez, and I am going to be your teacher." I smiled and shook her hand and watched as she walked down the row, handing out stickers to all the other kids.

After standing outside for what seemed to be an eternity, the bell rang, and one by one, I see the kids in front of me moving away from their parents and walking toward the building. My mother, of course, was one of the last ones to leave. She stood by my side the entire time, talking to me and telling me how much she loved me and how much fun I was going to have. My little black shoes walked in a line with the other kids until we finally reached the door, and I waved her goodbye and took my first step into this strange new building.

I was looking all over for a picture of Jesus somewhere since my mom and Doug told me that the school was going to be such a great place for me to learn more about him, but I did not see any. As we were walking down the hall together, we abruptly stopped at a wooden statue that was standing in a glass case in the middle of the hall. I looked at the statue, expecting to see Jesus's face, but I was surprised to see that it wasn't Him. It was a statue of some woman. It was a statue of Mary, the mother of Jesus, whom the school was named after.

Mrs. Hernandez said to everyone, "This is the holy mother Mary, and every day before class begins, we will be saying a new prayer to her called Hail Mary." Now I had been fully aware of the Our Father prayer, but I was confused as to why we were being taught to pray to Mary now.

I saw along the walls that there were pictures of every saint you could think of, and it wasn't until we arrived at our classroom that I finally saw a picture of Jesus nailed to the cross above the clock on the wall. I sat down in my chair next to some other boy who was just as nervous as I was being in this strange new place, took a breath, and said to myself, "Well, here goes nothing." The day seemed to fly by, and before I knew it, I heard my teacher Mrs. Hernandez say it was time for lunch—and the rest was history.

School in general for a five-year-old can be intimidating to say the least. But as time went on, I really began to like it there and all the new friends that I had made. Everything seemed to be going really well, except for having to wear those terrible uniforms, of course. I would come home from school, rip off that uniform, and hide it under my bed in case any of my neighborhood friends decided to stop in so I would not be embarrassed. When I told them I was going to St. Mary's and not Haldane, they all were confused and wondered why I wasn't going where they were going. But I just told them that my parents were making me. These discussions were easily cut short with the suggestion of playing football outside, and then it was back to normally scheduled programming as a kid.

Chapter 5

A Boy into a Man

One morning the telephone rang while I was busy watching cartoons and eating a bowl of cereal. My grandmother usually occupied 90 percent of our incoming calls, so I really did not pay much attention to it, thinking that it was probably just her calling to talk to my mom. My mother walked over, picked up the phone, and said, "Hello?"

Instead of hearing their everyday chitchat talk that I was used to, I was confused as to why all I heard was complete and utter silence. This was the type of silence where the world just seemed to stop. I looked up and saw my mother with this horrified look on her face that I have never seen before. She started crying, and all she kept saying was "no, no, no, this can't be" as her body slowly slid down the wall where the telephone was. She hung up the phone, and I ran up and hugged her.

"Mommy, why are you crying? Why, Mommy?" I asked her. She didn't answer me but just kept hugging me harder and harder as she cried on the kitchen floor. Her makeup was running down her cheeks from the tears, and I kept wiping them away with my hand to help her.

After a couple minutes had passed, she picked me up and said, "Mommy's okay, baby. Mommy's okay." Clearly, I knew she was not, but she didn't want to tell me what was wrong. "Go and get ready for school. We're going to be late," she said. I walked into my room and put on my uniform, confused and anxious to find out what was bothering my mother so much. We walked down the porch of our house and hopped in her car and drove off.

The next day I woke up and sat in front of the television like I normally did with my bowl of cereal and favorite cartoon playing. My mother walked by me and pulled out a chair from the kitchen table and sat down. She still looked upset from the previous morning when she had received that weird phone call, so I was keeping a close eye on her. She looked at me in the living room, sitting on the floor, and said, "Come here, baby, I wanna talk to you for a second." I noticed Doug was standing in the living room with a concerned look on his face as well that I just wasn't used to seeing on either of them. I walked over to my mother, holding my favorite action figure in one hand and a spoon in the other, and sat down in the chair next to her.

She looked at me and said, "You know how much Doug and I love you, right, baby?"

I said yes.

She said, "You know that we will always be there for you and will always love you, right, baby?"

I said yes.

She said, "Okay, well, I have something that I need to tell you, and I want you to be strong when I tell you this."

I said, "Okay, Mommy."

She said, "Daddy has died and has gone to be with Jesus in heaven."

I cannot think of a harder thing to do in this world than to sit your child down and to tell him that one of his parents has died. My mother was crying at this point, and I sat on the chair next to her, quietly trying to put together exactly what she had just told me.

I said, "So you mean your daddy died, Mommy? How did Grandpa die?"

In my mind, I could not fathom the thought that my father—who, at that point, was a young man—could have died, so the first thing that popped into my head was that my grandfather had passed away.

She looked at me and said, "No, baby, not my daddy. Your daddy has died."

This was the kind of news that no five-year-old child should ever have to endure, and I was forced to sit and listen to it.

I sat there and felt a wave of emotions come over me unlike anything that I have ever felt before in my short life. My stomach got very tight, and my hands started to sweat as the tears poured out of my eyes.

I said, "Well, how did he die, Mommy? What do you mean?"

She said, "Daddy was sick, baby, and had an infection, so God called him up to be with him so he wouldn't have any more pain."

Now the last time I had seen my dad was a couple months before this when he took me out for the day and bought me a toy, so I was confused because he seemed healthy to me. My mother was very vague in her description of what my dad had died from, and that was okay with me. I was not as concerned with finding out what he had died from. My mind was still trying to grasp the idea of him being gone and never seeing him again. Even though I had rarely seen my dad and we really didn't have a close relationship at all, I was still heartbroken.

The following Monday, my mother and I went to pick out a headstone for my dad's gravesite. I was still in shock from the news, but I am sure getting to miss a day of school did not bother me too much. I remember sitting in the shop where they were making headstones and talking with the woman as to what I wanted on my dad's grave. Picture a five-year-old boy looking at pictures of different options to use for his dad's headstone and being asked to come up with something to write on his grave. The woman had a whole book of headstones for us to look at. I flipped through the pages still numb to the fact that my dad was indeed dead and I was picking out what was going to go on his headstone.

The woman looked at me and said, "What do you think about this style, isn't this nice?"

I nodded my head yes, pretty much just so I wouldn't have to sit there any longer and look through the different kinds they had.

Then she asked me, "What do you want written on the headstone, hun? We can write whatever you like underneath his name."

I looked at the different font styles and sizes and told her that I just wanted it to read My Dad. Being as though my dad and I have the same exact name, it was weird to see Christopher James Maskey written on the grave with My Dad written underneath. My mother paid the woman, and we walked out of the shop, hopped in the car, and drove off. A part of me felt like I would never be the same again after that day. I felt like the innocent little boy inside of me had been forced into becoming a man before I was really ready to.

Later that night, my mother and I were watching television on the couch together when, suddenly, we heard a loud knock on the door followed by the screeching of tires. My mom went to answer the door, and to her surprise, there was no one there. She opened the door and looked up the street to see the taillights of a car driving off in a hurry. As she opened the door, she noticed a huge box was left at the bottom of the steps with a note that had my name on it. I went outside and helped her drag the huge box into our living room to see what exactly was in it.

My mother opened the box to find all my dad's personal belongings inside of it. Somebody must have boxed up all his things and decided to drop them off at his son's house for me to have. I looked inside and saw all his navy papers and pictures of him traveling around the country with his navy friends. I also found a ton of pictures of myself in there, which told me that he really did love me and always kept a picture of me close by. There was a box full of different coins from the different places he visited in the navy and a little gold cross that looked like it had seen better days. I found at the bottom of the box a little Bible that comforted me when I saw it, thinking that he was with Jesus in heaven and not in any pain. After we were done going through the box, I took a couple of my dad's belongings and kept them tucked away in my closet to keep in memory of him.

Since my dad died, we never once heard from his parents or anyone from his family—no card, no phone call, nothing. I had never even met my grandparents on my dad's side, and it seemed that even with him dead, they still did not want anything to do with me. They never even offered to help pay for their son's headstone, so if my mother had not gone ahead and bought one, he probably would not have had anything. I can remember feeling a sense of rejection. I felt unwanted while this was all going on. I could not understand how nobody on my dad's side wanted to be a part of my life. I was confused about how my mother's family loved me so much and always wanted me around yet my dad and his whole family never did. These are the kinds of things no child should ever have to deal with.

Chapter 6

Blinking Eyes

The following year, after my father had died, I noticed a change in me. I was still the happy-go-lucky boy that I always was, but something just felt different inside of me. I was getting to the age where I understood the things going on around me much better, and my mind was like a sponge taking it all in. My dad's death was a devastating part of my childhood, but having Doug and my mother there helped me to try to put it all behind me. My mother was concerned that his death would have a long-term negative effect on me, so she tried to take my mind off it by buying me things. I was a spoiled child before, but after he passed away, it was ten times worse. I must say it worked because I was so occupied with school, toys, and my family and friends that my dad's death seemed to fade away as the months passed by. I was ready to get my life back to normal again, or so I thought.

A couple months later, we took our weekly trip to my grandparents' house for Sunday dinner. I was anxious to get there to see if my cousin Tim would be there so we could play with our collection of G.I. Joes together. It was literally my favorite part of my entire weekend.

We pulled up to the house, and I did not see anyone's cars there. So I was immediately disappointed, thinking that I would not get to play with anyone. We pulled into the driveway, and I noticed that my grandmother had been standing in the front yard with her hand on her hips, anxiously waiting for us to get out of the car. She was smoking a cigarette and had a look similar to the same look my mother had a couple of months prior when she got that phone call about my dad. She walked over to my mom to talk, and I ran up the stairs to see my grandfather as I normally did.

I walked into my grandfather's room and saw him sleeping in his bed.

I yelled out, "Grandpa, what ya doing sleeping?"

I walked a little closer and noticed that his eyes were open, so I knew he wasn't sleeping.

"C'mon, Grandpa, get up. Let's watch the *Three Stooges*. I'm bored."

Still no response. But his eyes remained focused on the floor, and they were not moving. I walked over to him and shook him to try to get him out of bed but still his eyes did not move.

Suddenly my mother ran frantically up the stairs to where we were and put her ear on my grandfather's chest.

I said, "Mommy, why aren't his eyes blinking, and why is he just staring at the floor?"

My grandmother came up the stairs and stopped in the hallway, looking into the bedroom where my grandfather was lying. She was very cautiously looking into the room where we were, almost as if she was scared to walk past the entrance of the doorway.

She said, "He's dead, isn't he? Please tell me he's not dead."

My mother took her head off my grandfather's chest and started to cry, which then triggered my grandmother to burst into tears as well. I was literally frozen in the middle of the room. I couldn't believe that my grandfather had just died, and I was two feet away from his body. My mother told my grandmother to take me downstairs while she dialed 911, and we both walked down the stairs together. Little did I know that was the last time I would ever see my grandfather's face again.

Apparently, my grandfather had passed away in his sleep. My grandmother had been making him lunch and was calling his name for him to come down to eat it. After a couple tries and no response, that is when she went up there and found him. I felt so bad for my grandmother. They had been together for over forty years and had four children together. He was the love of her life, and she was his.

After the ambulance came, I sat on the couch with my grandmother while they ran upstairs with this big stretcher. A couple of minutes went by, and suddenly, I saw them come down with my grandfather lying on it with a white sheet covering his entire body. My mother followed behind and walked with them outside. I was sitting next to my grandma when she put her arms around me, and we both cried on the couch together. Moments later, Uncle Tim, my cousin Little Tim, Uncle Tom, Aunt Kathy, and my cousins Jamie and Jill all arrived at the house.

As I sat back on the couch watching my entire family walk in one by one crying, I couldn't help but think about my dad. I was wondering where he was exactly when he died, and did he die in his sleep peacefully like my grandfather did?

My mind was all over the place, and I remember feeling light-headed, so I went outside to cool off. My mom followed me out the door to make sure that I was okay. She said, "Grandpa's now in heaven, baby. Him and your dad are up there together."

I said, "I know, Mommy, I know."

She put her arms around me, and the dizziness I had suddenly went away. My mother had a way of doing things that just always comforted me and made me feel better.

After I walked inside, I noticed everybody sitting around the dining-room table and telling old stories of my grandfather and how funny he was. My mother told the story of how, one time, one of my grandmother's friends came over to their house fresh out of the beauty parlor, showing off her new hairdo. I was only a year old or two at the time, but apparently, she bent down to give me a kiss, and I turned the hose on and sprayed water all over her, ruining her new hairdo. She was so mad, and my grandfather picked me up and sat me on his lap and said, "Good job, little buddy. I didn't like her anyways!"

While the grown-ups continued to sit around and tell old stories, my cousins and I walked upstairs to where all the toys were. I remember slowly walking past Grandpa's room as if I was expecting him to jump out and scare us. As I was walking down the hall, I noticed all the pictures of Jesus that my grandparents kept on their walls, and I felt so comforted, similar to how I felt when I found my dad's Bible in the bottom of that box that was dropped off our porch.

We sat in the room with all the toys. But we could not force ourselves to have fun, so we all walked back downstairs.

My grandmother was sitting there listening to everyone's stories but didn't say much. I remember that out of nowhere, she came out and said, "Well, at least I know he's with GJ now."

Remember how I said my grandparents had four children? Well, my uncle GJ was the one that I failed to mention when I was listing the family members. My mother, Uncle Tim, and Uncle Tom had another brother by the name of GJ, who had been named after my grandfather. He had died many years back, before I was even born.

Apparently, he was walking by this little stream that was just two seconds from where my grandparents' house was and slipped and fell on a rock. He hit the back of his head on one of the rocks and eventually drowned there. I remember my grandmother would always look at the stream whenever we would drive past it but would never say anything.

It comforted my grandmother to say that GJ and my grandfather were together in heaven, and everyone agreed with her when she said it. This was the second time in my young life that I came face-to-face with death, and each time, I was comforted when the thought of this place called heaven was brought up.

A couple weeks later, my grandmother was in the same predicament that I was in the previous year regarding picking out what she wanted on her husband's headstone. She knew it would eventually be the place where she would be buried as well, so ultimately, she was picking it out for the both of them. I saw on this paper that she was drawing out a picture of herself lying under a tree with a book in her hand along with her dog, who was sitting next to her.

On the other side of the paper, she had drawn a picture of a man in a fishing boat trying to reel in a huge fish that he had just caught. It seemed to capture both of their passions in life: my grandmother loved her books, and my grandfather loved his fishing. She brought that picture to the shop that was making the headstone, and they created it exactly how she asked them to.

It made my grandmother feel good when she finally saw the finished product, and she said, "He's probably up in heaven right now just fishing off his boat and smiling down on me."

My mother smiled and said, "Absolutely."

Chapter 7

The Altar Boy

My years of attending school at St. Mary's just seemed to fly by for me. The gap between first grade and fourth grade had gone by in the blink of an eye, and I was soon approaching my tenth birthday. I was a good student but, at the same time, had slowly made a name for myself around the teachers' lounge as the class clown.

During the week, we would have designated trips planned for each class to take walks into the school's church for mass. I remember every mass was exactly the same every week, and at one point, I had memorized what everyone in the church was going to say before they even said it. Everything seemed very repetitive, and I remember not really taking a liking to going to church, which was odd for me being as I was so interested in learning about Jesus and loved him with all my heart.

A couple of months into the school year we were brought in front of the priest so he could discuss what we were going to be learning that year. He needed us all to pay attention to the steps he was about to teach us because we were about to finally make our communion. The Catholic church's sacrament for this was done by transforming a wafer chip and cup of wine into Christ's body and blood, similar to what Jesus had done at the last supper.

Apparently, it was a really big deal to all the teachers and people working in the church for us to be there and learn this. Obviously, for the children in my class, we had no idea what we were doing, and it seemed like the parents were more excited about it than any of the kids were.

During our training, we were taught all the different steps that we needed to memorize before the big day was here. There were specific ways we had to walk down the aisle and specific ways we had to put our hands out when receiving the wafer chip. The priest would then say "the body of Christ," and you would take it and eat it as you walked back to your seat. Apparently, it was to make you feel as if you had a piece of Jesus inside of you at the time, but to me, it was just a piece of wafer. I always felt like I had Jesus with me all day, every day, regardless and did not need to do this just so a man in a robe could tell me that Jesus is with me.

I remember talking to my mom and Doug about it, and both of them being Christians, they fully understood where I was coming from and agreed with what I was feeling inside. Still, due to my school's policy on it being a requirement to receive all these sacraments, I was told that I had to do it anyway. I swallowed my pride and kept my feelings to myself, but something inside of me was telling me that I was right for feeling the way I did.

Because of my newly developed reputation as the class clown, when we took these weekly trips to the church, I often found myself being forced to sit directly next to my teacher. I remember feeling really jealous that my whole group of friends got to sit next to one another and goof around while I was stuck quiet as a mouse next to my teacher. She purposely did this to keep an eye on me and to make sure that I was not getting preoccupied during these lessons. The priest would always look at me while making his speeches, and I could tell in his mind he was thinking, *That's got to be the infamous boy I've been hearing so much about in the teachers' lounge that likes to joke all the time!* I would sit there and act as if I was really interested in whatever he was speaking about, but really, I was just being polite.

The day of communion for my class had finally arrived, and everyone's parents were eager to go. We all arrived at the church one by one, comparing our outfits and going over last-minute procedures so nobody messed it up when we had to walk down the aisle. Some kids had their whole entire family in attendance, so you can imagine how jam-packed this church was. Families were posing for pictures and taking out their video cameras so they could capture every second of this so-called special day.

Now I do not want to come across as disrespectful or anything because I have the utmost respect for anything regarding God, but for me, this day literally had nothing to do with God and everything to do with the church and the parents of the children. So needless to say, I wasn't exactly thrilled about all the forced smiles and picture takings I was going to have to do following that event.

Before my communion was about to start, I noticed that a couple of my friends who were in the grade above me were at the church as well. I walked over to them, trying to stay away from the picture taking that was going on, and said, "Hey, guys, what you doing here today? I thought you already made your communion last year?"

My friend Johnny said, "Yeah, but we're here to be altar boys for the mass. Usually, for masses like this and funerals, we get paid a nice chunk of change!"

My eyes opened up, and I said, "Wow, really? They pay you guys to do that sometimes?"

Johnny said, "Yeah, well, it's usually the families who pay us if we do a good job during the mass. The best part about it is, a lot of times, they call us up during school hours and we get out of class!"

I was anxious to be involved as soon as I heard the words "out of class."

Johnny said, "They're always looking for help. If you want, I can put in a good word for you to Father." I took him up on his offer and told him that I was very interested.

The whole communion mass was very similar to the same boring weekly mass that I had memorized word for word, and besides our little walk down the aisle to receive the bread, it really wasn't much different.

Once the festivities were over, I couldn't wait to run over and meet my mother and Doug outside the church. Unlike every other kid who was bragging about how much money they were going to get and how many presents they were going to receive when they got home, I was pretty quiet and just wanted to get in the car and get out of there. I remember taking a picture with my teacher in front of the Mary statue in front of the church, and that was about it. We got in our car and headed home. I was anxious to see how much money and what type of presents I was going to get, just as did all my other classmates.

Looking back now, I realized that the whole communion process had nothing to do with God and what he wanted. Trying to find somewhere in the Bible where God said we needed this done was impossible to find, but nonetheless, I did as the church asked. It was really just another reason to have a party for the adults, and the kids loved it because we got lots of money and toys.

A couple weeks later, I remember seeing my friend Johnny in the hallway, and he asked me if I still wanted to be an altar boy. I said of course and told him to let me know when they needed me, and I would be there. Johnny found out that, apparently, they were short one kid for the mass that day, and they were really in a bind.

I told him I would do it, and he told me not to worry about anything. He would run me through everything before the mass started. In the back of my mind, I was thinking to myself about how I literally knew the entire mass procedure step by step due to seeing it every single week for the last five years, so explaining anything to me wouldn't be necessary. Even though it wasn't a wedding or funeral mass and I wasn't going to get paid that day, I was still pretty excited that he had reached out to me to get my foot in the door, plus that whole little thing about missing class for an hour I didn't mind either.

Two hours later, I heard my name, along with Johnny's name, called over the loudspeakers in my classroom, telling us to report to the church in thirty minutes for mass. My teacher looked at me with a strange look, almost as if to say "how did you swindle your way into this one?" I just sat there with a smile on, and when the thirty minutes was up, I jumped out of my chair and ran to meet Johnny. He was outside the church, waiting for me, and we both walked through the back entrance together to meet the priest. Because this was my first mass, Johnny told me that he was going to be handling the majority of the duties that the lead altar boy had to do, such as bringing up the bread and wine to the altar as well as ringing the bell when the priest lifted them up for the blessings. I was pretty much there for moral support and to get my feet wet on that day.

I remember sitting up on the altar during the mass and looking into the crowd. Nobody was really into the mass, and everyone looked like they were just there to say they went to church for the week. It was sad to think that in the house of God, nobody was really getting anything out of it. The small handful of people who were responsive during the mass would get up and say the same repetitive prayers, always really loud and obnoxious. It was as almost as if it was done just to show that they fully knew the prayers and to stand out in the crowd. I doubt anyone really thought about what they were saying or what the priest had them repeating. It was like watching a room full of robots, to be completely honest.

I sat back watching them throughout the entire mass, thinking to myself that something just felt wrong. There were statues of Mary and other saints scattered throughout the altar, and I remember thinking to myself, *Why aren't they just praying to Jesus? Why are they praying to all of them and not Him?*

After the mass was over, I went back to class and sat at my desk. I could not get out of my mind what I had just witnessed. There's a big difference between sitting in church and only paying attention to what's in front of you and being on the altar and getting to look into all the people's eyes as the mass is going on and see what they are getting out of it. From that day on, I always had a chip on my shoulder when it came to going to church and listening to the same repetitive prayers to Mary and the other saints. Jesus is what I needed, and I did not need to jump through burning hula hoops to get Him.

As time went on, I continued to do my duty as an altar boy and continued to see the same results from the people attending mass. After the sacrament of communion, we were now on the verge of our confirmation and reconciliation sacraments that the church deemed necessary for us to complete. I remember confirmation was another man-made ritual that had no biblical relevance, but still, we did it as the church asked.

After confirmation was a sacrament that really bothered me, and I will never forget how uncomfortable it was when I was forced to do it. It was the sacrament of reconciliation. For those of you who aren't aware, reconciliation was when all the kids were forced to walk into a dark room separated by a thin wall where one of the priests was sitting on the other side, awaiting the child to confess to him what sins they had done. Talk about uncomfortable for a little kid to be sitting there, telling this strange man hiding behind a black screen all his/her sins.

After the child was done, the priest would then acknowledge the sins, and he would tell the child an appropriate punishment for the child to do that would wipe away the sins. Usually, the punishments were in the form of repeating some repetitive prayers. The day of my reconciliation I had gone in there and told the priest some of the things I had done, not really being 100 percent honest with him. And frankly, it was none of his business in the first place.

After I told him what sins I had done, the priest paused for a second and said, "My son, I would like you to go home today and repeat the Hail Mary prayer twenty times and the Our Father prayer fifteen times. If you do this, your sins will be forgiven by God."

I went home that night and told Doug and my mother what had happened during my turn for reconciliation and what the priest had told me to do to make up for my sins. I remember Doug looking at me and going, "I just want you to be fully aware that you can confess your sins to God anytime you want, pal, and you don't have to do any of the things that the priest told you to do today."

I had gotten the answer I was looking for regarding how I felt about this situation, and my mother fully agreed with this too. I felt as if saying the Hail Mary prayer two hundred times was ridiculous and would not change anything in my life, regardless of what that priest told me.

Again, this was just another ritual created by the church that was not scriptural, but nonetheless, we were forced into it. I had, at this point, already established a relationship with the Lord and was accustomed to praying to Jesus and asking for forgiveness in my life. All the added steps that were told to me that day were confusing and, in reality, were completely wrong.

Chapter 8

That One Summer

My time as a student at St. Mary's Catholic School was coming to an end. I had been there for nearly seven years, and I was anxiously awaiting the next step in my life. Besides the whole reconciliation ritual and a few other things that were odd to me about the school, I really did have a good time there. I had just turned eleven years old and was a couple of weeks away from graduating from St. Mary's. This would then mean that I would finally be going to Haldane, where all my friends from home had been attending this entire time. I would be starting all over again in a brand-new school and leaving behind all my friends that I had been with at St. Mary's. We all were on the verge of moving on to the infamous junior high school.

The summer after my graduation from St. Mary's, I really had the time of my life. We had a group full of neighborhood kids that all stuck together the entire summer. I figured this was a good time to really get close with these kids being as I'm going to be going to school with them in the upcoming year. Justin and I had still been really close, and he was still pretty much a part of the family. Instead of playing with toys and video games like those that we used to play with, we were now into nothing but sports all day, every day. Basketball, football, baseball, hockey—pretty much anything that involved running around and being competitive, we were into.

My mother and Doug both worked full-time, so I was home alone during the day without a care in the world other than having fun. Usually, as soon as one of us would wake up, the chain of phone calls from kids willing to come outside and play would begin.

My good friend Jeff, who lived down the street from me, had a basketball hoop in his driveway, so I would just open my window and listen to see if I heard a basketball being dribbled to know if he was up yet or not. This was way before the time when everyone had cell phones and could call at any minute. I would walk down to his house, and we would start shooting hoops to wake us up in the morning. As we were shooting, it was not uncommon for other kids who lived close by to come join us one by one as they heard us playing. By noon, there were usually twenty kids or more in the driveway, shooting around and playing two-on-two tournaments. I really had a group of friends that I fit in well with and that accepted me even though I was the kid who attended the Catholic school.

The daytimes during that summer consisted of football and basketball, and by nighttime, we were always playing "manhunt." Manhunt was a game that both guys and girls could play, usually consisting of a group of kids broken up into two teams, trying to hunt down and find one another hiding in the dark of the night. On any given night, it would be an understatement to say that we had a small army of kids rampaging up and down our two-block radius.

I always remember my mother would be driving up and down the streets looking for me, and if by chance, she happened to see me in the midst of the sea of other children, she would call me over to the car and say, "Chris, it's late. Tell everyone good night and you'll see them tomorrow."

Of course, I would bargain an extra five minutes out of her, which would then turn into an extra two hours. But she knew how much fun we were having, so she wasn't too mad.

Some nights my mother would walk down, sit on the sidewalk, and hang out with all the kids as we were playing. As soon as someone saw her come down, you would hear the kids yell "Karen! You're on my team!" She was really loved by everyone, and she just had that personality that was different from most of the other parents on the block. She was cool! She was always allowed to come and join our games while any of the other parents would have been forbidden!

My mother was my best friend, and she was never, for a second, too busy to not take part in whatever was in her son's life. It was a fun time in my life, and that summer before I started going to junior high will always live in infamy on our street. I'm sure the neighbors were glad when we finally got back to school so they could go to bed early and didn't have to worry about the loud screaming or the occasional ding-dong ditch that went on for the entirety of the summer.

That summer was also known for the classic Little League baseball games that the kids put on. Being as the town was so small with not much to really do, everyone came out and supported us kids as we hit the field every weekend.

I can remember spending hours outside with Doug, throwing the ball around and trying to build up my fastball and get ready for the upcoming season. Doug had signed up to be a part of the teams' coaching staff, and him being a baseball junkie, you could tell he was really into it. He even umpired some of the games after mine was over, so it was pretty much like a second job for him being involved in our league. I loved pitching, and I jumped at any opportunity my coach had opened for me to hit the mound.

My mother was, by far, my biggest fan, and her voice could be heard miles away, cheering me on as I was on the mound. One kid even asked me if I was ever embarrassed at how loud my mom would be cheering, and I remember laughing and saying, "Nope, that's just how my mom is."

Doug was competitive as well, but he did it in a more controlled way. We always had our little talks following the game on ways I could have improved my performance that day. Pitching really came naturally for me, but I am sure all the late-night catches with Doug had a lot to do with that.

The night following one of my games, my mother would always buy the newspaper so she could cut out all the clippings with my name in the highlights and save them. She had a whole collection of sports articles with my name in the highlight page somewhere. She even saved the articles where I would go one for five, and when I would ask her why she was saving that one, she would say, "Hey, at least you got a hit!"

Playing baseball was a good way as well for me to make friends with the kids whom I was about to go to school with after the summer was over. After the games were over, we would all go to whoever's house had the nearest pool and celebrate. This summer always stood out to me over all the other ones because of the new friends I made and the fun we all had.

This summer was the beginning of many new things in my life. My uncle Tim had just remarried, and his new wife already had a son named Mikey, who just happened to be the same exact age as I was. Whenever we took our weekend trips down to my grandmother's house, I would get a chance to play with my cousin Tim and now Mikey as well. The three of us got real close, and we ended up spending a lot of time together that summer. My cousin

Tim was a couple years older than Mikey and I, so he was always one step ahead of us with everything. This was the summer that I would really get hooked on a certain genre of music—rap music.

Hip-hop had taken over the '90s, and my cousin Tim brought it directly to both of us. Even before that summer, I always remember being drawn to that type of music, but this summer, I was officially hooked on it. The lyrical content was intense, and the sounds that would come out of my cousin's boom box were dark and intimidating for a young kid to hear. My new cousin Mikey was also really into it, and we would have long talks on what albums we liked better than others. My mother hated me listening to it, and often times, my cassette tapes just happened to disappear without her ever knowing where they went. She used to tell me that the music was filth that was from the devil, and she would do everything in her power to try and stop me from listening to it. Unfortunately, there is only so much a parent could do, and ultimately, she couldn't prevent me from turning into an all-out hip-hop fan.

I noticed the more I was listening to the songs, the more and more I wanted to emulate how the rappers were acting and how they looked. The majority of my friends back home really weren't into what I was bringing over to listen to, but they would eventually fall victim to it the more I would play it for them.

My clothing attire did a complete 180 as well. I went from wearing Nike shirts to Tommy Hilfiger and Polo. My jeans went from Levi's to Boss jeans. I was rarely seen without a baseball hat on that was always turned to the back.

I was hypnotized from the whole movement, and my cousins were too. We would even get together and write our own rap songs on the weekends. I quickly found out that there is not much an eleven-year-old boy from Cold Spring could really rap about.

Unfortunately, for me, the subject that I knew the most about, which was my love for God, really was not something that would have been accepted by my friends or considered cool in a rap song. So I decided to start copying what all the other rappers were saying in their lyrics when I would write my own. It was violent, it was sexual, and it took over the majority of the kids I knew back then. How coincidental that it was just in time for junior high school to start.

Chapter 9

The New Kid

Summer had finally ended, and I was days away from starting at my new school. I pretty much already knew everybody that would be there between living in a small town all my life and playing sports, so school wasn't as intimidating for me as I'm sure it was for any of the other new kids who knew nobody there. I was coming from a strict Catholic school, which gave us no freedom at all, to this public school that was literally two minutes from my house that I could walk to if I wanted. This was not just a new school; this was junior high school. Graduating from St. Mary's and finally stepping into junior high was a big deal, and all my friends were just as anxious as I was to get there.

My mom was visibly more nervous than I was on the morning of my first day. She kept asking me if I knew where all my classes were and how I was going to get home after school was over. My mother was always overly nervous over things like this, and I could not help but tease her about it. She would say, "Okay, so you got your keys, and you're going to walk right home after school, right?"

And I would say back to her sarcastically "I don't know. I may walk home. I may just end up catching a ride out of state to a huge party. I haven't decided yet."

My poor mom never thought it was funny, but it made me laugh every time when I would joke with her like that.

Doug was always the calming factor in the house when my mother would have her unwarranted panic attacks. He would walk up to me and say, "Good luck today, pal. You got this!" It would drive my mother nuts to see how calm he was about things while she was so nervous. We would often team up and push her buttons just to see how far we could get. That morning though we decided to take it easy on her since she was so nervous about me starting at my new school.

I will never forget the feeling that I felt walking through the doors for the first time. The halls were packed with kids making noise and talking with one another, and it looked like a scene out of the movie *Animal House*. It was something that I was not used to in my old school where everyone was pretty much quiet and kept in order. I remember walking over to the first familiar face I saw and starting to talk to them to try to blend in.

Even though everyone somewhat knew me from town or playing sports, I still had all eyes on me when I walked through those doors. I thought it was so cool that the school even had a soda machine in the hallway since my last school had nothing of the sort. It felt good knowing that I would never have to wear those ugly uniforms ever again and I had full control over what I was going to wear every day. I stood there talking to my friend for a couple of minutes, then I heard that infamous bell ring, and off I went.

School was always pretty easy for me as far as comprehending the material. At St. Mary's, I always got pretty good grades, and most of the time it was with minimal to no effort. When I actually tried on an exam that I wanted to do good on, I would ace it with no problem. My only issue throughout my entire time in school was staying motivated and paying attention. I walked into my very first class at my new school, and it was intro to Spanish. I had already taken Spanish for two years at my old school. I knew this class was going to be a breeze for me since I already knew all the materials, so it was going to be tough for me to stay attentive. I paid attention the first couple of minutes but quickly lost interest and started resorting back to my old routine of making people laugh. The class clown in me came back in full force.

Being the new kid in school, I tried to get as many people as I could to like me so I would feel accepted. The schoolwork took a back seat to my jokes and off-the-wall behavior that I would use to try and reel in the other kids to notice me.

Throughout my entire first day, I did nothing but try to impress people by goofing off in class. I can remember one of my teachers telling me, "It is going to be a long year, Mr. Maskey, if you keep up this kind of behavior."

I was like an animal that had been locked in a cage for seven years being released in a mall full of people. My old school had us under such strict rules and regulations that when I got to junior high, it was like a whole different world to me.

After my first day was over, I ran out the door and started to walk home for the first time. I had never felt this much freedom before. I was thirteen years old, but I felt like had jumped straight into manhood that day. When I finally got back to my house, I kicked back on the couch and started watching the television. Two and a half seconds later, the house phone started to ring.

"Gee, I wonder who this could be," I said sarcastically to myself, knowing that my mother would be calling to make sure I got home all right.

I picked up the phone and said, "Hello?"

My mother was waiting on the other line. "Hey, Mr. Big Shot, how was your very first day at your new school?"

I laughed and said, "It was great. Everybody was really nice, and I did really well in all my classes."

Knowing full well that I was already on the radar with all my teachers as being a potential troublemaker, I didn't find it necessary to tell my mother that at this point.

She said, "That's great. I'm so proud of you! I knew you were gonna love it there."

I said, "Yeah, it was a lot of fun, Mom. I think I'm gonna do good too."

In the back of my mind, I was having flashbacks of all the chaos I had caused in the classrooms that day and would laugh at how naive my poor mother was. I just said, "Yeah, Mom, I had a really great day today, and I can't wait to go back tomorrow." In all honesty, I really could not wait to go back the next day. However, it was for all the wrong reasons.

It only took a couple weeks until the whole "new kid" tag was off me, and I was viewed as just another kid in the school. My best friend, Justin, was in the grade above me, but we always remained close during our years in school together. We did not have any classes together, but news of my immediate impact on the junior high teachers spread fast. He would get a kick out of it all.

Throughout that entire year, I was pretty much a regular in the lunch-detention and the afternoon-detention crowd due to my behavior. My time in class was focused more on having a good time and making people laugh than it was on my schoolwork, and I quickly learned that it was not going to be tolerated. I do not know if it was just an age issue or if it was because I was new to the school and desperately wanted to fit in, but it's safe to say my mother wasn't too happy with how my new school was turning out for me. Through the years, I managed to control my behavior in class better (but still had my moments), and I breezed through my junior high experience with no problem.

As fast as junior high came and went, it seemed that high school went by even quicker. All the homecoming games, dances, and friends that I had made through the years were all coming to an end right in front of my eyes. Before I knew it, five years had gone by, and I was approaching my senior year of high school. I could tell my mother wasn't in any rush for me to graduate. If it were up to her, I would be five years old and playing with toys in her living room forever. I was her only child, and the thought of me growing up and leaving home really upset her. I had one year left—my senior year—and it would turn out to be one of the toughest times in my entire life.

Chapter 10

The News

Walking into school for the first day of my final year of high school was much less intimidating than it was when I had started back in the seventh grade. I did not have to worry about fitting in or making new friends; all I had on my mind was to have a good time and to cherish the last moments I would have there.

I had just gotten my license that summer and had bought my very first car, a 1996 Honda Civic that I would parade around town every night to show off to my friends. It was not anything flashy, but for a seventeen-year-old kid, it did not matter as long as you had a car. I had been working at a local video store for a couple years for some extra money along with Justin and a group of my good friends. I had a girlfriend who I was in a serious relationship with and a ton of good friends to occupy my free time. Life was going great for me.

One afternoon, a couple of months into my senior year, I was sitting down with my mom watching a movie, as we would usually do, when I noticed something was troubling my mom. She had gotten up from the couch and gone to the bathroom a couple times in a row, but I paid it little mind. Only when she had gotten up for a third time in a row and closed the door to the bathroom did I get worried and walk over to ask her, "Everything okay, Mom?"

She opened the door with this look of concern on her face that I will never forget, and she stood there looking into the mirror.

I said, "What's wrong, Mom? Tell me."

She turned around and said, "I'm fine. I just don't know what this is in my mouth."

She turned around and opened her mouth for me to see, and I noticed there was a white lump that was starting to form on the side of her mouth. It was bigger than any canker sore I had ever seen, and I could tell from my mother's facial expression that she was visibly scared of what it could be. I looked down at her and saw she was still smoking a cigarette even after finding this lump that was growing on the side of her mouth. I walked over and took the cigarette pack that was on the table and crushed it and said, "You better put them cigarettes away before you make it any worse!"

She knew I was right and immediately put out the cigarette. She walked over to the sink to get some water and mixed salt in it in hopes of helping with some of the discomfort she was feeling. I told her that she needed to call a doctor and get it looked at immediately, and she agreed. She sat back on the couch with me, but it was obvious she could not concentrate on anything other than what she had just shown me.

The following week, my mother made an appointment to finally see a doctor. Upon her visit, the doctor immediately recommended that she have a biopsy performed so they could rule out exactly what was growing in her mouth. She came home afterward and was in good spirits, saying, "I think it's probably something silly like an allergy, or maybe I burned myself from the soup the other night."

In my heart, I was praying that she was right, but something deep down told me it was going to be bad news. After the biopsy was done, we all sat around the phone that night anxiously waiting to hear the results so we could go on with our normal lives. My mother had convinced herself that it was nothing and that she was going to be fine in a week or two. Doug tried to have a positive mind-set too, but you could tell he was just as concerned as I was.

Suddenly, the phone rang, and my mother jumped off the couch to go and pick it up. She answered the phone, saying hello in a confident voice, and stood there ready for the news that she was going to be just fine. I noticed that something was terribly wrong just ten seconds into the conversation when her eyes filled up with tears, and she looked absolutely terrified. My stomach was in knots, and I immediately began to feel nauseous. She sat listening to the phone for what seemed an eternity, listening to the doctor tell her what he found in the results. I walked over to her, waiting for her to hang up the phone to tell us what he said, but in my heart, I already knew. She hung up and immediately fell into my arms and started to cry. Then out of her mouth came the news that no kid ever wants to hear his or her parent say. She mustered up enough energy and said, "It's cancer!"

We all sat around my mother hugging her and reassuring her that everything would be okay. This was the first time ever that someone I had known had been diagnosed with the dreaded C word, cancer. This was not just anybody, but my mother—my rock, my best friend. She was everything in my life, and she was now sick with a deadly disease.

Back then, all my knowledge in regard to cancer was very limited. All I had known about it was that it was related to smoking and that it was a killer, but I had no idea what kind of monster it really was. My mother finally wiped away her tears and sat back on the couch with us. She told us that the doctor wanted to try something called *radiation treatments* on her in hopes that it would shrink the tumor. I told my mother that whatever she needed to do, I would be there for her through it all, and we were going to beat it! We had to beat it. I was just about to start my life, and I could not imagine going forward without her with me.

A couple weeks later, we had gone with her to start her first round of radiation treatments. In that small length of time between doctor visits, the tumor had already grown, and I was concerned that they were not being aggressive enough. I remember my mother would hold my hand so tight when we walked through the hospital doors. She was absolutely terrified at what was awaiting her behind those doors that none of us were allowed to follow her into. The process of her radiation consisted of them making a model cast of her entire face followed by her lying still on a machine that would be burning her mouth with radiation rays trying to kill the cancer cells and shrink the tumor.

After the first treatment, she walked out of the door with this look on her face that I will never forget. The combination of the pain she had felt from the radiation and the internal terror she was experiencing had left her with a blank stare on her face. She was trying to be strong and not to show us that she had been mentally defeated until we reached the car, and she broke down and started to cry hysterically. These radiation treatments went on for months, but the months seemed like an eternity. Watching the person you love more than anything on earth suffer like she had was the worst thing I've ever had to go through in my short life.

Throughout the entire treatment, I witnessed my mother demonstrate what the word *faith* was really all about. She was scared, no doubt about it, but because she fully placed her trust in Jesus and what His plan was going to be for her, she had a sense of peace about her through it all. I would often wake up in the early morning to go to the bathroom and would see her up reading her Bible and highlighting certain scriptures that would give her help along the way. One passage that I always remember that she would keep close to her was Psalm 27:1, "The LORD is my light and my salvation—whom shall I fear? The LORD is the stronghold of my life—of whom shall I be afraid."

She would literally live out that same scripture every time she would go to the doctor's, walking in with a smile, knowing that whatever God's plan was, she was okay with it. I remember being so proud of my mother and how brave she was throughout the entire time battling with this disease. Her love for God and her faith in what Jesus did for us on the cross led her to a place where nothing was intimidating to her anymore; she was prepared to face whatever God had decided for her.

The doctors decided that the amount of radiation she had received had reached its maximum amount, and it was time for phase 2. At this point, the tumor had grown in size and had now spread to the back part of my mother's tongue. She came home one day after her doctor's appointment and sat Doug and I down to let us know what they had told her. She told us that they wanted her to go down to the city for four days to have a special procedure done that would target the exact location of the cancer and should produce better results. She was nervous about the procedure, but she had been through so much already that she seemed a little more at ease this time around.

My mother told me that if she went and had this procedure done, I was not allowed to go with her and neither was Doug. She wanted me to stay home and concentrate on my schoolwork, but in my eyes, my life as a senior in high school was already over. I was a full-time caretaker and motivator to my mother in this battle we were all a part of, and instead of worrying about getting my grades up and concentrating on which college I wanted to apply for, I was consumed with what was going on at home.

Nonetheless, my mother gave us her ultimatum and told me that she was going to go with Marie, her best friend, who lived across the street from us. Being as it was only for a couple days and she was going to be with Marie, I agreed to stay home and concentrate on school along with Doug.

That night I sat with my mom as we packed her bags for her upcoming trip to the hospital in the city. She was putting in her clothes along with a big book of crossword puzzles that she loved to do to pass the time. Before we zipped up the bag, she hopped up and said, "Oops, I almost forgot the most important!" She walked over to her nightstand and came back with her Bible and placed it ever so gently on top of everything else in the bag and then zipped it shut.

I said, "Are you going to be scared, Mom? I hate the fact you're not letting me come with you down there."

She looked at me and said, "Of course I'm scared, who wouldn't be? But as scared as I am, I find comfort in knowing that I won't be alone at all, and God will be there with me through it all."

The following day we said our goodbyes, and off my mother and her friend Marie went. Before she left, she kissed me on my cheek and said, "Now go hit those books and study hard for your mom!" All the things going on in this poor woman's life, and her main concern was me focusing on my school grades so I could get ready for college.

As Doug and I sat in the driveway waving her goodbye, I felt as if I was in a dream and that this whole thing was not real. Just a month ago, we were laughing with each other on the couch; now my mother was in a car on her way to New York City to help fight off her cancer. I always hated the fact that she smoked so much, but the thought never even crossed my mind while growing up that she would get cancer from it. I guess, until it happens to you and your family, you never really think something horrible like this could happen to you.

Her procedure was scheduled for one o'clock that afternoon. Doug and I sat patiently in the living room, waiting for the phone to ring to let us know how it went. A couple of hours later the phone rang, and it was my mother's friend Marie calling from the hospital.

She said, "Hey, Chris and Doug, your mom is out of the surgery, and she wanted me to call in and let you know she's okay. She can't talk because they needed to perform a tracheostomy on her, so she has the tube in her throat right now. She wanted me to tell you she is going to call you later and communicate with you by pushing the buttons on her phone. One beep means yes, and two beeps means no, okay?"

I sat there sick to my stomach at the thought of my mother lying on a bed with a hole in her neck and a tube sticking out of it, unable to talk to us. I could not fathom the thought that now she was going to have to communicate with me all week by pushing buttons on her phone to answer my questions.

I said, "Okay, well, please tell her I love her and I miss her. Tell her I can't wait for her to come home!"

We hung up the phone, and I walked back into my room and broke down on my bed feeling so helpless that I could not protect my mother from all this.

Later that night, the phone rang. It was my mother. I picked up the phone to hear a nurse say, "Hello, is this Christopher? I am with your mother right now. She wanted to talk to you. As you know, she cannot talk because of the trachea, so she will only be able to talk to you by pressing buttons on the phone, once for yes, twice for no. Okay, here she is."

I sat there and heard nothing but silence, wishing my mother in her calming voice would just come out and say something. I finally said, "Hey, Mom, you there? I love you so much."

All of a sudden, I hear the beep from the button on her phone. I am sure it broke her heart to not be able to tell me that she loved me too and that all she could do now was hit a button on her phone.

I said, "How are you feeling? Are they taking good care of you down there, Mom?"

Another beep came through the phone.

I continued asking her questions and telling her how much we all loved her for a couple more minutes, until her nurse came back on and said she was going to sleep for the night. I told her to take good care of my mother and that I would call her in the morning.

The next couple of days, we continued calling each other and communicating through the phone with the beeps. It was the fifth day that she had been gone, and my mother was now finally scheduled to come home. I was so anxious to see her and just give her a kiss and hug her. Doug prewarned me that she was probably going to be weak and that we really needed to keep an eye out for her when she got home that day. I remember seeing her friend Marie's car pull up the street and pull into our driveway. I was finally getting my mother back. I ran outside and stopped in the driveway, waiting for her to get out of the car, but I was not prepared for what I was about to see.

She opened the door, and my heart just dropped as she slowly got off her seat and walked out of the car. It looked as if my mother had aged twenty years in those five long days, and for the first time, I could see the effects of what this cancer was doing to her. She had a bandage over her neck, covering up the hole from the trachea that was removed from her throat. Her face was white as a ghost, and it looked as if she had lost a lot of weight since I had seen her last. Not to mention they had removed the tumor and part of her tongue, so her mouth was bandaged up as well. It was the scariest thing I had ever seen in my life, to see my best friend like that. We helped her out of the car and walked her up the stairs back into our little house where she belonged.

Chapter 11

Remission

The worst part about living with someone you love that has cancer is the uncertainty. The months of radiation and the surgery that my mother had gone through were all done in hopes of healing her of this disease, but none of us knew what the future would hold. I would often pray to God in my room at night, asking Him to rid my mother of all her pain and make her healthy again because I knew, if anyone could do this, He could. We had our share of good days, but the majority of the time, I would wake up in the early morning to my mother crying in severe pain. I would feel guilty even eating in front of her because she was at a point where all she could eat was soup due to the doctors removing part of her tongue and due to the hole in her neck from the trachea. My mother stayed positive and told me not to worry because Jesus had a plan for everything and she would be fine, no matter the outcome.

As time went on, we would see my mother, little by little, regain her strength. She was fully recovered from the trachea and was even able to eat some soft food. She was gaining weight, and for the first time in a long time, it felt like my mother was winning the battle.

One weekend we went over to my grandmother's house for dinner just as we used to do every weekend before she got sick. As soon as I walk in the door, I see my grandmother lighting up a cigarette on the couch. I could not believe my eyes when I saw this. My mother was literally fighting for her life because of her years of smoking, and my grandmother continued to smoke as if nothing had happened. My mother waited in the other room for her to put out the cigarette, and then we walked into the dining room together. It is hard to imagine someone sitting in a room with his/her child missing part of his/her tongue and with a hole in his/her neck all caused from smoking and continuing to smoke right in front of him/her. It was at that point that I realized the addiction to smoking cigarettes had my grandmother full force, and she had no intention of letting it go.

The school year seemed to fly by during my senior year, and we were finally approaching the big day. Graduation was something that my mother had talked about with me since I was a little kid, and I could tell how excited both she and Doug were for this. I was just happy that my mother was getting healthier and our lives were slowly getting back to normal again. My grades were okay but not great, so it was obvious that I would not be attending Harvard that upcoming school year. I decided to apply to a couple of local colleges in hopes that one of them would accept me, which would be a good thing to stay local because then I could still be close to my mother. I did not care where I went just as long as my mom was alive and well. I was determined to do good wherever I went.

One day I came home from school, and my mother was sitting on the couch with a handful of mail on her lap. She sat there trying to act as if she was not excited, but I could see it in her face that she was hiding something.

I said, "Is that the mail from today, Ma?"

She smiled and looked up at me with a huge grin and said "yep, let's see what we have here . . ." as she thumbed through the mail, stopping at a bright-blue envelope that was last in line.

She said, "Well, would you look at that? You got a letter back from one of the colleges you applied to, Mount St. Mary's."

My mother would always make the biggest deal out of the littlest things and was always so proud of everything I did. It was not as if I had an invitation to attend Yale or an Ivy League school, but to her, she was so proud of me no matter what.

I opened up the letter and was instantly relieved when I read the first three words—Congratulations, Mr. Maskey—and found out that I was accepted!

My mother sat there with a smile on and said, "Well . . . what did it say?"

Of course, I had to mess with her and I said, "Nope, I didn't get in, Mom."

She got up and came over to hug me and said, "No big deal, Chris, you're gonna get into something better I'm sure anyways."

I sat there laughing and then told her that I was just kidding and that I really did get in. You would have thought she hit the lotto with how happy she was. I mean

I was happy too, but she was kissing me and hugging me as if I just won the Nobel Prize or something. Doug, of course, was just as happy, but he did not find the need to carry on as she did, and he came over and congratulated me as well. Both of my parents were real supportive of me in whatever I did. I think, because of what we, as a family, went through that last year, it was even more special for them though to find out that I still made it to college and that we overcame this obstacle together as a family.

On the night of my graduation, I was just as anxious as my mother was the entire time. I remember standing up on the podium, sweating as I waited for my name to be called, so I could walk up and receive my diploma. As soon as I heard my name, I walked up, took my diploma, and then looked into the crowd. My whole family was in attendance, standing up and cheering for me, along with Doug and my mother.

Doug had his video camera out, filming the entire thing, and then I looked to the left and saw my mom. She was clapping and yelling just as she had done all those years when I was a little kid on the mound pitching in baseball. I looked at her face, and I couldn't help but get choked up thinking about all that we had gone through that year and how much she fought to be there that day. She had fought so hard and had been through so much, mentally and physically, but today was her day. She had on the biggest smile that night, more than anyone else in the whole entire building. Her only son was officially graduating and moving on to bigger and better things in life, and she just had to let the world know how proud she was of me.

As proud of me as she was that night, I was just as proud of her. She was the one who deserved the standing ovation and clapping from everyone, not me. To overcome cancer and be in remission was no easy task, but we fought together as a family and made it through. That night was a celebration not just of me graduating high school but a celebration of my mother in her victory and eagerness to keep on living life. Before I walked off the stage that night, I waved to my mother in the crowd, and she smiled back at me with tears in her eyes and said, "We did it!"

Chapter 12

The New Me

College had finally arrived, and I was more than excited to move out and finally be on my own. Mount St. Mary's was literally only twenty minutes away from my house, located in the city of Newburgh. Even though the college was so close to home, I still decided to live on campus so I could get the full experience of it all. Needless to say, my mother wouldn't have argued with me if I had decided to live home and just commute there, but she understood that I wanted to be on my own. So she went along with it.

I pulled up to the freshman dorm room and walked through the door to find an empty room with two bunk beds on each side of this tiny room. This meant I was sharing a room with three other people, and I wasn't thrilled about that being as the room was so tiny. Since I was the first one there, I had dibs on which bed I wanted, and I quickly ran over and took the bottom bunk and put all my bags on it. My mother and Doug were looking around the room, wondering how in the world four people were going to coexist in this tiny space.

As the day went on, my three roommates arrived one by one, and we got to finally meet one another. They all seemed like nice kids, and we all shared the same concerns for how small the room was.

My mother and Doug stayed for a little while then gave me a hug and left. I remember my mother saying, "You are gonna do great. I know God has big plans for you, son!" On his way out, Doug gave me a hug and told me, "We're fifteen minutes away if you need anything, pal. Love ya." And then they both walked out.

As soon as our parents left, we unpacked our things and tried to get to know one another a little more being as these were the people we would be living with from now on. This went on for about an hour more, then it was time to head off to our freshman orientation and thus start our careers as college students.

As the weeks went by, I slowly became more and more used to the fast-paced life of being a college student. I always made sure I came home every weekend to stop in and see my mom and Doug and check up on how my mother's health was. My mother, being in remission, was cancer-free, but she still continued to go back for tests every couple of months to make sure that everything was okay. She would always be anxiously waiting by the door when I would pull up in the driveway and would then run out and give me a hug and kiss the moment I got out of my car. I know it was tough on her having her only child away at school, so I always made sure I called her a lot and came home to visit as often as I could. We would still take our trips on the weekends to my grandmother's house for her famous meatball wedges and for us to spend some quality time with my family, then I was back to my tiny dorm room.

One weekend I came home and surprised my mom and Doug for the weekend. I parked the car in the driveway, and two seconds later, I saw the door slowly open. My mother wasn't expecting me, so she carefully opened the door to see who it was when she heard my car door open. When she saw it was me, she got all excited and ran down the stairs to hug me. Doug was in the backyard working on cleaning the pool but was also really happy to see me when I went back to see him. It always felt good to be home and away from the nonstop chaos that college life can bring. As soon as I got there, my mother sat me down and made sure she cooked us all a nice dinner.

That night after we all ate dinner, I sat with my mom on the couch, and we watched a movie together. It was great spending time together like the good ole days when we would do this as a kid. After the movie was over, my mom asked me, "So how's everything with school? How's life living on your own, Mr. Big Shot?"

I laughed and said it was okay and that I was doing really well in my classes. She smiled and said, "I'm so proud of you and the man you've become, Chris. You're gonna be great in whatever you do in life, I just know it!" She was always so positive, my mother, and I could always count on her for some needed encouragement whenever I was home.

That night we ended up talking for hours about anything and everything. For some reason, the topic of my biological father came up, and I started asking questions about him. My mother, for years, had always just told me he had gotten sick but was very vague on what exactly he had died from, so I never really pressed the issue my whole life. I decided that night was going to be the night when I found out the details on what happened exactly, and I wasn't ready at all for her response.

"So, Mom, what exactly did my real dad die from? I know you always told me he was sick and went into the hospital, but you never really told me with what."

My mother looked at me with a troubled look in her eyes and said, "Well, I've been dreading you asking me this question for eighteen years now, and I think it's time that we talk about this, son. Before I go on any further, I just want you to know how much he loved you and how much you meant to him, Chris."

At this point, I was extremely confused as to where she was going with this, and at the same time, I started getting the "butterflies in my stomach" feeling again, anxious to hear what she had to tell me. She grabbed my hand and said, "Your dad was involved with some of the wrong people and got into using drugs and drinking a lot, and apparently, they found him dead in his apartment with his wrist cut."

I said, "So he killed himself? My dad killed himself? Is that what happened?"

She shook her head and said, "I don't know what happened, baby, but you need to know how much he loved you and how much you meant to him. He was going through a tough time in his life, but honestly, I don't know happened other than what I was told."

My mind was beyond racing at this point. Everything I thought I had known about my dad and his life up until this very moment had changed. To think that he would take his own life was shocking to me, as it would be for any kid to come to grips with. It brought me back to that time as a kid when someone knocked on the door and just dumped off the box full of his belongings on our porch. I also started thinking back as to why all these years had passed and I still had never met any of his family or anyone on his side. The pieces were starting to come together, and all the weird things that happened as a kid now were making sense to me. My father had apparently committed suicide, and as a kid, there couldn't be anything more disturbing to hear than that.

I lay down that night and tried to go to sleep, but I couldn't. My mind was all over the place, reliving old memories and then picturing what my mother had just told me over and over in my head. A part of me wished that I had never gone home that weekend and even asked about it. I wished I was still under the assumption that he had died from being sick instead of the heartbreaking news that my mother had just told me.

The next day I woke up and saw my mother reading her Bible on the couch. This was nothing out of the ordinary as she was always reading it and highlighting certain passages that she really liked. Having cancer had really drawn my mother to her Bible even though she had always been a woman of strong faith, just like Doug was a man of strong faith. I walked over to my mom and sat next to her on the couch.

She put her arm around me and said, "Are you okay, hun? I know what we talked about last night was tough for you to hear, but you can't let something like that ruin your life and let it stop you from what you set out to do. You know, whenever you feel down or need someone to talk to, you can always pray to the Lord, and He will be there for you."

I nodded my head and said "I know," but like most eighteen-year-olds, I didn't really fully understand how important having that relationship with Jesus really was.

Ever since I was a kid, I had always had an interest in learning about the Bible and growing closer to God. My mother and Doug tried to keep that a main priority in my life, but sad to say, through the years I really got farther and farther away from Jesus. I always believed in Him and loved Him, but I was more focused on my life and what was going on around me than I was on getting closer to Him. When I had learned about my mother and her cancer, I definitely prayed to God a lot, asking Him to heal her and to help me deal with the emotional stress I was dealing with at the time.

As a believer, I was always fully aware of there being two places we are to go to once this life is over. We either go to heaven to be with Jesus or hell where we will suffer for eternity. Now, in my mind, I had always pictured my dad being in heaven. I know he had his share of problems, but growing up under the impression that he had just simply died from being sick, I always pictured him up in heaven with Jesus. Now that I had learned the truth about what really happened, I started to question whether or not he really made it to heaven. The thought of my dad being in hell burning in fire was something that I couldn't get out of my mind.

Later that day, I gave my mom a kiss and hopped into my car and drove back to college. Instead of taking my mother's advice and sitting down to pray for guidance on how I could deal with my problems, I decided to just bury them deep inside and numb myself with alcohol. College was the perfect atmosphere for that, and it quickly brought me to a place where I didn't have to think about everything bad in my life. As time went on, I pretty much found myself using alcohol more and more frequently, to the point where I was drinking every day. The problems in my life weren't going away, but the drinking made them seem like they weren't even there.

My freshman and sophomore years of college flew by, and I was on the heels of starting my junior year at Mount St. Mary's. My grades were still good, but at this point, school had no longer been about my grades and getting a college degree for me. I was more concerned with partying.

Initially, I started drinking to take my mind off my mother's health problems and the news of my dad's apparent suicide, but I found myself drinking so much at the time that it was tough to even function sober. I would find any and every excuse as to why it was a good time to have a couple drinks and would look for anyone to hang out with that had the same mind frame as me. Besides the drinking, I was smoking weed every day and trying other drugs as they would come along. For the average twenty-year-old college kid, I guess this was the normal, but I was, by far, using them much more frequently than anyone I knew.

One Friday night, during the beginning of my junior year, I walked home from class anxious to get back so I could crack a beer and get the weekend started. I walked up and noticed my mother and Doug were sitting in her car parked in front of my dorm. My mother was in the car, and she told me to get inside because she wanted me to come home for the weekend and spend some time with them. I knew something was up, so I ran upstairs and got my clothes and jumped into the car with them.

My mother was in the passenger seat, and she was real quiet the majority of the ride. I leaned over to her and said, "What's wrong, Mom? Why are ya being so quiet, and why did you insist I come home this weekend?" At first, she didn't answer me, and all I heard was her nose sniffling as if she had been crying and was trying to cover it up. Then, out of nowhere, my mother said, "I have something to tell you, Chris. Your grandmother passed away today."

Now I had just spoken to my grandmother a week before on the phone and literally had no idea she was even sick at all. I do remember talking to her, and at the end, I said, "I love you, Grandma, see you soon." But when I said it, she didn't respond back like she normally would, and it seemed as if she was crying on the other end of the phone. But I really didn't pay it any mind.

I said to my mom, "What do you mean she died? I just talked to her on the phone last week! What happened?"

My mother, at this point, was crying, and she said, "She had cancer, and it was extremely aggressive from her years of smoking. They tried to help her, but the doctors said there was nothing that they could do."

The same nauseous feeling that I had felt over and over in my life was once again back in full effect that whole ride home. My grandmother and I had been so close throughout the years, and it was too much to handle for me to think that not only was she gone but that I also never got to say goodbye to her and give her one last kiss. Doug and my mother tried to comfort me by saying that she was at peace with the Lord now and she was in heaven, but at the time, I couldn't feel any comfort at all. I sat back the whole ride to their house, replaying old memories of my grandmother in my head and what an important role she played in our family.

As soon as we got to the house, we all hopped out and hugged one another in the driveway as a family. I know it was tough on me and Doug, but my mother had just lost her mom, and you could tell that it had affected her tremendously.

Later that night, we sat down to eat, and I noticed my mother wasn't really eating. She had a plate of food in front of her but wasn't really touching it. I figured because of the sudden death of my grandmother that she probably just didn't have any appetite to eat. When dinner was over, I sat beside her on the couch, and we began to talk. I asked her if she was okay and why she didn't touch her food at all during dinner. My mother looked at me, and I could tell something was wrong.

She said, "I don't know what to do. I think there's a couple more small tumors in my mouth, and I'm terrified to go and find out what it is."

She opened her mouth to show me, and my heart broke yet again. I figured that since my mother had been in remission from cancer for nearly three years, we were over it for good, but I saw a couple of little tumors that were starting to form along the front of her gumline and in the back of her mouth where the original tumor had been.

I said, "Mom, how long have you noticed them there? You need to go to the doctor's and get them taken out!"

I could tell from her facial expression that she just didn't have any more fight in her from all the pain and discomfort she went through in her first battle with cancer. But she told me she would go to the doctors and get them looked at soon.

The following week, she went to the doctors, and they recommended that the tumors be removed immediately before they grew any bigger. This was a same-day procedure, and she would be back in a couple of hours, but she would have to go back to the city at the infamous Sloan Kettering Cancer Hospital. My mother told me not to miss class, and that she would be fine driving down with Doug and that she would call me as soon as her procedure was over.

I remember sitting in class, not being able to concentrate on a word the teacher said from being preoccupied thinking about my mom. I looked around the classroom at all the kids taking notes and getting involved in the lecture, and I remember wishing that I could just trade places with any one of them for a day and not have to live in constant fear, worrying about my mother. I would get sick to my stomach to the point I would have to get up and walk out of the class to the bathroom at just the thought of my mom dying. It was my biggest fear, and I struggled with it every day of my life back then.

The bell rang, and I ran to my dorm room anxiously, awaiting a phone call from Doug to let me know how the procedure went. I remember sitting in my dorm room alone and praying to Jesus that He would comfort her during the surgery so she wasn't scared and that He would guide the doctors during the procedure. A couple of minutes later, my phone rang, and I was happy to see the name Mom pop up on my screen.

I answered it, and she was on the other end in good spirits, surprisingly. I said, "How ya doing, Mom? Everything go okay? Are you in any pain or discomfort?"

She said, "No, just a little tired, but I'll be home shortly so I can lie down and rest when I get home."

I told her that I would meet her at the house and drove home to see her.

That night, she came home, and I saw Doug helping her out of the car. So I ran over to give him a hand and to give her a hug and kiss. She was so happy to see me, and I was just as happy to see her. Doug told me that they removed the tumors, and we would find out shortly the results from the biopsy that they had done. My mother looked happy that the tumors were removed, but I could tell that she wasn't too optimistic for good news on the upcoming test results.

She looked at me and said, "Well, babe, we did all we could. It's all in God's hands now. I just pray that it's not cancer again. I can't go through what I went through last time again!"

I helped her into the house and said, "It'll be better news this time, Mom. I just know it!"

She smiled, and we sat on the couch together. But a couple of minutes into me being there, she ended up falling asleep. I could tell she was exhausted, so I helped her get comfortable on the couch and laid her favorite blanket over her. I thought back to all the years my mother took care of me and did this for me when I was sick as a child. Now it was my turn to take care of her just as she had done for me my entire life.

The next couple of weeks I was back at school, but I really was of no use in class. The stress of dealing with my mother and her health, the loss of my grandmother a month before, and the thoughts replaying in my mind of my biological dad killing himself were enough to make my head explode. The old, happy, and fun-to-be-around Chris was gone, and I didn't like the new me.

My mother would always tell me when times were tough to pray to Jesus, and He would comfort me in my time of need. But instead of taking her advice as usual, I decided to drink away my problems. I would even drink by myself many nights, just sitting in my dorm room alone, trying to block out what was possibly coming. The thought of my mother dying was something that went through my mind 24-7, and it got to the point that unless I was drunk, I was unable to even function. I slowly stopped going to class as frequently as I normally would, and college had turned into just a place for me to go to sleep at night after my binge drinking.

The following week was Thanksgiving vacation from school, and I went home to spend it with my mother and

Doug. Now this was the first Thanksgiving we had ever spent without my grandma and her cooking, so nobody was even excited about celebrating. Plus my mother was still recovering from her surgery. She was in no mood to even look at food because of the pain she was still in. I told Doug that I didn't want to eat either because I would feel terrible eating food in front of my mom while she sat there in pain, feeling miserable. He agreed and said that would be wrong of us to do, so for the first time in my life, we were going to just not have a Thanksgiving dinner due to the circumstances.

Thanksgiving Day had come, and I remember sitting in my room and hearing Doug start up his car and seeing my mother and him get inside together. I was puzzled as to where they were going, but I figured she had errands or something to do that day so that's where they were probably going. About a half hour later, I saw Doug's car pull back up, and I watched him help her out of the car and walk back up the stairs. I noticed my mother had a bag with something in it, and I was wondering where, exactly, they were coming from at this point.

I walked out of my room to meet them in the living room, and I noticed my mother was in pain. Doug helped her onto the couch, and she was complaining that her mouth was in terrible pain and she just needed to rest.

I said, "Where did you guys go? You should have been resting all day, Mom, not out doing errands."

Doug took the bag out of her hands and showed me what's inside. I looked and saw that it was turkey and mashed potatoes from Boston Market.

Doug said, "Your mother felt bad about us not having any Thanksgiving dinner this year, and she made me drive her to Boston Market so she could buy us food to eat."

I looked over at my mom, and she smiled at me as she sat down in pain on the couch. I thought to myself that even at this very moment, while she was suffering in pain and unable to eat anything, all she cared about was that her son and husband have food for Thanksgiving. That's just who my mother was; everything she did in this life was for others, with no thought of herself, ever. I sat beside her and gave her a hug and kiss and thanked her for the food, but it was clear that nobody that Thanksgiving was going to be able to enjoy anything while Mom was in pain.

My twenty-first birthday was slowly approaching, and I told my mother I was going to come home from college that night to see her. She told me she wanted to give me some gifts and her homemade card that she gave me every year. On the day of my twenty-first birthday, I drove off to see my mom and Doug and also to check up on my mother and her health. I had also made plans for later on in the night with a couple of my friends who were home at the time and who were going to take me out for my birthday after I visited my mom and Doug.

I got to the house and saw my mother standing in the doorway, waiting for my car to pull up so she could come outside and hug me. I pulled into the driveway, and before I could hop out of the car, she was there waiting for me.

"Happy twenty-first birthday, my son. I love you so much. How's it feel to be twenty-one?" she asked as she hugged me.

I told her I loved her too and told her to hurry up and get inside so we could get out of the cold.

We sat on the couch together, and I could tell she was very emotional that night. She kept talking about all the childhood memories we all had together and how proud she was of me. Seeing me turn twenty-one was a big deal to her, and she was never one for holding back her emotions when it came to her love for me. Doug walked in the door and gave me a big hug and wished me a happy birthday as well and sat on the couch with us. I told them I was planning on going out with some friends that night to celebrate, but I wanted to hang out as a family the following day so we could do something fun. Midway into our conversation, the phone rang, and my mother, as usual, got up to answer it.

I continued to talk to Doug, not paying attention to who it was that my mother was talking to on the other line. Our conversation was quickly cut short at the sounds of my mother crying out "no, oh please, no! This can't be, please no!" We both immediately jumped off the couch to see what was wrong and ran over to her. My mother was in tears, losing her balance as she was standing, listening to whatever the person on the other end was saying to her.

She hung up the phone and began to cry on my shoulder as I walked her over to the couch to sit down. She looked up with tears in her eyes and said to Doug and me, "That was my doctor telling me the test results of the biopsy! It's cancer again! But the worst part is, the doctor told me that the results showed that it's an extremely aggressive form of cancer this time! He said I have to have my jawbone removed, and they need to cut off part of my leg bone to replace it! I can't do this. I just can't go through with all this!"

The terror that ran through my body at that moment was something I will never forget. We went from being happy and talking about my birthday to receiving a phone call with the worst possible news ever. My mother wept on the couch as we both hugged her, and I couldn't help but cry like a baby too. The three of us had been through so much in the past three-and-a-half years, battling this disease, and it seemed like the fight was slowly coming to an end.

I looked at my mother and said, "Mom, I know you're scared, but you have to get this surgery done. You can't just give up. You have to fight and get better!"

She looked at me and wiped away the tears from my eyes and said, "I'm so scared. I don't want to die. I need to be there for you! I can't die just yet. You're too young for me to leave you. It's not fair!"

I told my mom not to worry about me. She needed to concentrate on herself, and we both reassured her that we would fight this thing together as a family. As time went by that night, she slowly calmed down, and we all stayed together on the couch talking about everything that we just found out. My mother went from being scared to somehow talking positively and that she was going to fight this disease one more time!

She said, "I have something on my side that cancer doesn't, and that's Jesus!"

I wish I could say I was happy to see her anxious to fight back, but I couldn't help but feel lost in it all. I decided, at that moment, that I wasn't going back to college anymore that year and that I was going to stay with my mother and Doug to fight this thing together. I called up my friends and told them I wouldn't be going out that night for my twenty-first birthday and that I was going to be spending it at home with my family. My mother fell asleep on my shoulder as Doug and I sat on the couch with her, trying to stay as positive as we could for this upcoming battle we were about to face again.

Chapter 13

The Battle

Living at home was a big change from how I used to live back at college. I told myself I would take a semester off to be there for my mother, and when she got healthy again, I would go back to school and get my degree. Even through the news of how aggressive this new type of cancer was, we still remained confident and trusted in the Lord to get us through it all. The tumors had been removed from my mother's mouth just a couple of weeks prior, but I was now starting to see them form again, and she was in severe pain every day from it. I would often wake up early in the morning to the sounds of her crying in pain, and I would go to comfort her as best as I could. One morning the pain was so bad that she cried out, "Please take me, Lord, I can't keep living like this!"

Her surgery was scheduled for late December, and it could not come any sooner. At this point, the tumors had doubled in size, and my mother was literally scared to wake up and face the day every morning because of the pain. She was well aware of what the surgery entailed and how dangerous it was to perform. The doctors said they needed to remove her jawbone, take out the cancer that had grown back, and then remove part of her leg bone and replace it where her jaw had been.

She said to me one night, "I'm so scared to get this surgery, Chris. I don't want to die, but I can't live like this anymore. I will do this surgery for you and Doug, but I don't know how much more fight I have left in me."

We would have these talks every night it seemed, and it never got any easier seeing my mother scared like that.

Leading up to the surgery, my mother was concerned that the date it was scheduled for was only a couple of days before Christmas. She didn't want to spend the holidays in a hospital bed. I remember her telling me that she was going to postpone the surgery until after Christmas because she wanted to be home for it, and even though I knew we needed to get this done immediately, I couldn't tell my mother that she couldn't spend Christmas in her home.

At this point, my mother was skin and bones from not eating, and her diet consisted of soup and Ensure protein shakes. This was the worst time in my life, and when she would fall asleep, I would sneak off to the corner store to medicate myself with a twelve pack of beer. Trying to come to grips with what we were dealing with was extremely hard on all of us, but instead of trusting in God like my mother and Doug did, I chose to remove it all from my mind with drinking. My mom, throughout that entire month, was glued to her Bible, and I would see her taking notes and reading nonstop. She had been consumed with faith, and all her fear of the surgery and the possible outcomes just seemed to slowly go away because of it.

Christmas that year seemed to come and go all too quick. Much like our Thanksgiving that year, it was pretty tough to sit down and celebrate anything while Mom was fighting for her life and just days away from going through this life-threatening surgery to help and save her. She still wrapped my presents and sat on the couch with me while I opened them, excited to see my response. Doug and I helped her to open her gifts because she was too weak to even open them. She started to cry when she saw the one gift that I had made for her, which was a personal letter that I wrote to her telling her how much I loved her and that I had framed. She hugged the framed letter that whole day and kept reading it to herself and smiling. We all sat together in the living room as a family that day, not sure if this would, in fact, be the last Christmas we would spend together as a family.

The day before the surgery, Doug and I helped her to pack her bags and get ready for the hospital. She wrote out a list of all the things she wanted inside of the bags. On the top of the list, I remember she wrote "Bible, framed letter from Chris, etc, etc." She knew she was going to battle for her life, and she was armed only with a letter from her son and the Word of God. It had been a couple months since my grandmother had died, and it was still very fresh on all our minds. That night we sat up talking together about old times and reminisced about all the fun things we have done together through the years as a family.

She said, "Ya know, you have really been the best son a mother could ask for. Thank you for always being there for me. No matter what happens, my son, just know that I am right there with you in life and I will always love you, Chris."

I told her how much I loved her and how important she was in my life. I did my best to try and maintain a positive approach throughout the conversation and made sure I reminded her that she was going to beat this and get well again. She had to get well again.

The next morning we woke up at 5:00 a.m. and packed the car, ready to head down to Manhattan for her surgery. My mother slowly walked around the house, almost as if she was getting one last look at everything, before she walked out the door. My uncle Tom decided to come along for the surgery, so we waited for him to show up, and then we got in the car and slowly drove off down the road.

As we passed our house, my mother said, "I love our little home, but I think this is the last time I will ever see it." Tears started rolling down her cheek as we drove off on our way to the Sloan Kettering Cancer Hospital. Doug had known the way down there like the back of his hand from the numerous trips they had made for her checkups, but my mom was in no hurry to get there. I remember my mom kept asking on the trip down, "Are you sure you packed my Bible? I hope you didn't forget that." I knew reading her Bible was important to her, but I couldn't fathom as to why she was so enthusiastic about it being in her bag.

We arrived at the hospital and helped my mother out of the car and walked in. As soon as we walked into this hospital, my stomach was in knots looking at the patients. This cancer hospital was filled with patients who were battling this deadly disease, many of who were missing limbs. It was the scariest walk of my entire life, and I wouldn't wish that on my worst enemy.

After walking down the crowded entranceway, we made it to the elevator and got my mother to her pre-op room. She was in a lot of pain that morning and was tired from the walk to her room, so she was anxious to finally sit down. The nurses were telling my mother about the surgery and that, in total, it was going to take around eight hours to do.

We got her ready for surgery and made sure that she saw that her Bible was nice and safely put on the shelf in her room, which really comforted her. We gave her one big family hug and said a prayer together that God would take all her fear and doubt away and that He would guide the doctor's hands during the surgery. I gave my mom a kiss on the cheek and told her how much she meant to me and that we would be right in the waiting room for when she was coming out. She smiled and kissed me back and said, "God's got this, Chris. I'll be fine!" They slowly wheeled her away, and I noticed right before they got to the door that she stuck her arm out with the thumbs up, and then before I knew it, the door closed behind her.

I couldn't help but get emotional when I saw her being wheeled away. My mother, a shell of the person I remember growing up, was being taken into the operating room where they were going to take out her jaw and cut part of her leg bone off and put it back in her mouth after the tumors had been removed. To say I was stressed out was an understatement, but for some reason, my mother had seemed very calm about it all.

We went into the waiting room knowing that we were about to have the longest eight hours of our lives ahead of us. We sat down together and tried to occupy ourselves with the hospital's magazines as best as we could. I could not help but keep picturing my mother and remembering how brave she was going through all this and still maintaining her cool. Flashbacks of old memories that we had were replaying in my mind, and the thought of waking up one morning without my best friend there was making me sick to my stomach.

About an hour into the surgery, out of nowhere, we heard over the loudspeaker our names being called up immediately to the same floor my mother was being operated on. Immediately, my heart stopped when I heard my mom's name. The surgery was scheduled for eight hours, and here we were being called up already just an hour and a half into the surgery.

My heart was racing as I ran down the hallways, thinking to myself that something had to have gone terribly wrong. I remember saying, "Please, God, just let my mother still be alive. Please, God, I need to see her again." I walked up and was greeted by the nurse who told me, Doug, and my uncle Tom to please wait in a tiny little side room for the doctor to come in.

I paced back and forth in that tiny little room for what seemed an eternity, anxiously awaiting the doctor to tell me what was going on. All of a sudden, the doctor came in and sat down in the chair next to us. He came right out and said, "There is nothing we can do, guys.

The initial plan of removing her jawbone and the tumors was stopped by my personal decision after we opened her up and saw the amount of cancer that was inside her. I didn't want to put her though that long, painful surgery knowing that it wouldn't help her chances of ever beating this anyways."

The words that came out of his mouth hit me like a ton of bricks, and I remember not being able to breathe at that moment. I fell to the floor and realized that our positive thoughts on my mother having victory over this disease were over. Doug immediately came over and hugged me as we both came to the realization that our lives would never be the same again.

The doctor told us that my mother was being stitched back up and that she would be in the recovery room very shortly. I remember waiting in the hallway for someone to come over and tell me she was awake so I could run over and see her. I don't think reality had fully set in yet in my mind, and I was pretty much just running on emotion at the time. To hear the news that the situation was so bad that the doctors refused to even operate on your mother was something that none of us were prepared to hear; but

I was just thankful my mother was still alive, and God had answered my prayers.

Shortly after receiving the worst news imaginable that they couldn't help my mother in her battle with this disease, we were told she was awake in the recovery room. So we went in immediately to see her. I walked past a row full of cancer patients recovering from major surgery, all fighting for their lives, and finally made it to my poor mother. She was lying on the bed, and I noticed she was still very much sedated. We walked over to her, and I hugged her immediately and gave her a kiss on her forehead.

She looked at me and said, "How did I do? Is it all better now?" My heart broke at that point. Obviously, the doctors hadn't told her yet that they couldn't perform the surgery and that there wasn't anything they could do to help her.

I looked at her with tears in my eyes and said, "You did great, Mom. You did such a great job!" She smiled at me and closed her eyes and went back to sleep. I had no idea how I was going to tell her the truth, so I went into the other room and prayed for the strength to tell her and that God would take away any fear that we were all going to face.

We waited patiently in my mother's room for her to be moved after being in recovery. The doctor came in and let us know he was about to bring her in, and that, in fact, he had spoken to her.

I asked the doctor, "So did you tell her what happened and why you didn't do the surgery?"

He told us that he told her everything and that she was fully aware of everything at this point. I was so nervous to see her and what her reaction was going to be. How do I tell my mother that I know she's about to die and even the doctors admit there is nothing that they can do to stop it from happening?

Moments later, the nurses wheeled her into her room, where we all were, and I could see it on her face that she was upset. She looked at us all sitting in her room and started to cry as we ran over to her and hugged her. It's one thing to battle this disease with some sort of plan from the doctors on how to battle it; it's another thing though to hear the news that the battle is over. All we had at the moment was the present time before the cancer would take her life away.

I told my mother that the doctors had plans on something else to give her some hope, but the truth was there wasn't anything that the doctors could do to stop the inevitable. I remember having to go to the bathroom a couple times that day because I was sick to my stomach at the whole situation.

We sat with my mother until visiting hours were over that day, and I remember her being extremely upset when we finally had to leave. She was placed on a floor in the cancer hospital that was for the terminal patients and was now facing the fact that she was going to die in that same hospital at some point. I kissed my mother on the cheek and told her how much she meant to me. She smiled, and as we all walked out the door, I noticed her reaching for her Bible. She sat in that terminal floor hospital room not watching television or eating to take her attention off what was going on but was reading her Bible, preparing herself for when God would call her home.

I remember walking down that hallway that night emotionally drained and in disbelief of how the day turned out. We went into this day thinking that the doctors were going to do the surgery and remove the tumors, then after a while, she would be okay. But that never happened. I cried the whole way home that night, trying to envision how my life was going to be without my best friend there with me, and it was too much to handle.

When we got back to the house, I immediately ran to the store and bought some beer for the night. Instead of being strong and relying on Jesus to give me strength during these hard times, I chose the bottle to try and hide my problems, just like I did for everything else wrong in my life. I felt like a coward sitting there, drinking as fast as I could to take my mind off things, while my poor mother was sitting in her room reading her Bible, trusting in God to help her through this situation. Doug also went to his Bible when we got home and spent the rest of his night reading it while I sat in the next room drunk and by myself.

The following day I woke up in a room full of empty beer bottles with a severe headache. The alcohol had worn off, and the reality of my mother's situation was slowly coming back to me. Drinking never eliminated my problems. It simply just put a gap in time for me to forget them. But once I was sober again, the problems would hit twice as hard as they did the day before.

As time went on, we would go and visit my mother every chance we could get. As her health seemed to fade, her spirit seemed to get stronger, and her outlook on the situation was filled with less fear. It seemed as if she was fully accepting the things to come, and her faith in Jesus was the reason for it.

She was more concerned about me than she was for herself. I think she saw how emotionally drained we all were and how it was affecting me. She would make me promise her that I would always trust in God and go to Him for anything in life, but at the time, I just said it to make her happy. All I wanted was for her to be healthy and to come back home, but as time went on, I started to realize that was never going to happen.

Toward the end of my mother's life, the cancer had finally spread to her brain, and she was slowly losing her ability to say or do anything. I walked in one day and saw her on the bed lying there still and not moving at all. Her heart monitor showed she was still alive, but the cancer had now taken away her ability to move or communicate with us.

I walked over to her and took her hand and said, "It's okay, Mom, you can stop fighting. Go home to be with Jesus. You don't have to keep fighting. Go be in peace."

Doug and I walked out of the room that day knowing that we would never get to talk to her again. This deadly disease was slowly consuming her, and now it was just a matter of time. I went home and prayed to God that night that He please take her so she would not have to suffer any more. I could not bear to see her suffering any more.

The following morning, around 5:00 a.m., I heard our house phone ring. Without even getting up to hear who it was, I already knew that my mother had died. Doug answered the phone, and twenty seconds later, he came into my room and said, "Mom's gone to be with Jesus. The suffering is over."

I wanted to cry, but I do not think I had any tears left in me after the battle we had been through this whole time. I sat in my room, staring at a picture of her and imagining what she was doing up in heaven. Her faith in going there and how much she loved God eased my mind, knowing that she was, without a doubt, in peace with the Lord. I was picturing her up there, smiling with my grandma and grandpa in her new body, cancer-free, and in glory. I had literally spent twenty-one years on this planet with her side by side with me every day, and at that moment, I was finally feeling what it was going to be like to not have her around. It was a cold, empty feeling that I just could not get rid of no matter what I did. My mother was now gone, and Doug and I had been forced to pick up the pieces and start a new life for ourselves, without her.

That morning Doug and I sat in the living room, going through pictures and sorting out all her hospital papers that we had. I remember looking over and seeing Doug crying while he was reading this one paper in particular. I asked him what he was reading, and he showed me. It was a letter that he had written to my mother about fifteen years ago begging her to quit smoking. I started tearing up just reading it, thinking that if she would have listened and put those cigarettes down, she would probably still be there with us.

As I was going through her papers, I found one of her bibles that she had been highlighting different passages in as she was battling with cancer. As soon as I opened it up, one of her tiny folded notes fell onto the floor in front of me. I reached down to open it up and saw that inside she had written the same passage that she used to say all the time when talking about her cancer. It was Psalm 27:1, which said, "The Lord is the strength of my life; of whom shall I be afraid."

My mother used this quote in particular throughout her entire battle with cancer, and it was almost as if she wanted me to see it one last time to let me know she was not scared and that God was with her now. She was so brave and never once questioned why she was going through it; instead, she used this quote to motivate her to be strong when she was often scared and weak. She was not scared of death, and her faith in this quote showed that perfectly.

We had to have a closed casket at my mother's wake. The cancer had taken over her mouth and inside to the point that we could not even have one last look at her during the ceremony. The line of people who had come to pay their respects was down the block, which gave Doug and I some comfort in knowing how greatly she was loved and how many people she touched during her short time on this earth. I sat there in a trance during the ceremony, pretty much in disbelief that everything was happening. I had a one-track mind and that was, as soon as it was over, I needed a drink.

Before the wake was over, I noticed that my old kindergarten teacher from St. Mary's School was there with her son. Her son was a couple of years older than I was, and I had not spoken to him in years. But we were friends from when we both went to school together. He came over to me and gave me a hug and said, "Call me in the morning. I have a job for you if you're looking for work, Chris." I took his phone number down and thanked him for coming. I hadn't given much thought, at that point, to my future and what I was going to do. But I knew my days as a student were pretty much over, so I was going to need a job.

That night, after the wake was over, I went home and drank the night away, sitting in my room alone and thinking about my mother. Doug would come in and check on me from time to time, but I kept telling him I was fine just so I could get back to drinking. I walked by a couple times on my way to the bathroom and saw Doug in his room reading his Bible that night. He was just as upset as I was, but instead of drowning himself in a bottle of alcohol, he did like my mother and went to God for strength. I remember wishing I were as strong as he was and didn't have to drink all the time, but in my mind, it was the only thing that I thought would help me forget about how depressed I really was.

Chapter 14

Getting Tired

The weekend after we had buried my mother, I decided to sit down and figure out exactly what I was going to do with my life. The house was so quiet without my mother around, and Doug and I were going to have to get used to living our lives without her. This was the first time that the two of us would endure her absence in our home. I was now a twenty-one-year-old college dropout with not much job experience and was slowly walking down the road of becoming an alcoholic. I looked at the majority of my friends who were still in college or had graduated already and realized that I needed to do something with my life. I always thought in the back of my mind that I had to make my mother proud in whatever I did, and whatever road this life took me, I vowed to make the best of the heartbreaking situation.

I decided to call my friend Chris, who had offered me a job to come and work for him when he came to my mother's wake. It meant a lot to me that he even showed up since I hadn't seen him since my days back at St. Mary's. Now I was being offered a job at the lowest point in my life. This was something that I never expected but was appreciative of. Chris owned a company that installed low-voltage wiring to newly built homes and commercial buildings. I did not know much about the profession to be honest, but I was eager to learn and was just happy to be a part of something. He told me I could start the following Monday, and for the first time in a long while, I was happy about something.

I let Doug know that I had found a job much sooner than expected. He was really happy for me when I told him the news. Doug was working at a Party City store after IBM had its massive layoffs years earlier and was doing whatever he could to pay the bills and keep food on the table. Because my mother had accumulated over a million dollars in hospital bills and not all of them were covered by her insurance, Doug had the responsibility of not only keeping the house going but dealing with the hospital bills that were continuously coming in. Money was tight to say the least, but we were going to do our best to get through it together.

That following Monday I started my new job with Chris and was very anxious to start. I hopped into the work van that morning, Chris introduced me to the other employees, and off we went to the jobsite. There were two other people who worked for Chris, and they all seemed pretty close to one another. But they all welcomed me into the team with open arms. The first couple of days, I pretty much just followed Chris around and watched as he showed me what to do and how to do it. I had a general knowledge of how running telephone/cable wire was done. I picked up the daily job very easily. Before I knew it, I was on commercial jobsites, working hard and loving every minute of it.

The job took my mind off everything during the day, but at night, when I would come home, the old feelings of emptiness would pour in like a river. Walking up the front stairs and not having my mother waiting in the doorway to greet me and to give me a hug was painful. I would often get out of work and go directly to the bars to start drinking so when I went home later on, I would be intoxicated and not have to deal with the pain I was feeling. Some nights I would stay up all night partying and then go right to work with no sleep. I constantly needed to keep my mind busy. I did not want to stop and think about all that I had just gone through, so when I was not working, I was at the bar. At twenty-one years old, I thought I had all the answers to my problems. I really believed that, and as long as I did not have to think about them, I was okay and they would eventually all go away.

I was a hard worker and always gave it my best even though some of the days I was dragging from the partying from the night before. Chris was a great boss to work for, and he never really scolded me for coming into work hungover. I think he could see that the alcohol was starting to control my life, but because my mother had just died, he never really stepped in to try and get me to stop. I would come home from work and see Doug sitting in the living room, watching these preachers on TV talking about Jesus and how He could help you out in your life. I never lost my faith in God through it all, but I honestly never took the time to sit and listen to what

Doug was watching. We were both going through the same internal struggle, living without my mother, but we had different ways of dealing with it.

As time went on, I continued to work for Chris and learned all the ins and outs of the job. I became accustomed to waking up hungover and going to work that it did not even seem to bother me anymore. The majority of my paycheck every week was spent at the bar or on beer, and I was totally dependent on drinking to get through the week. Chris would often laugh at me because he would have to spot me money for lunch for the week because I had blown everything I had that weekend out partying.

I was living paycheck to paycheck, and the excessive partying was dominating my life. I was slowly losing control over my drinking even though I told myself it was okay because I could quit whenever I wanted to. Some mornings I would be so sick that I would not make it in to work, and then I would have to drink just to take away the feeling of being sick. Chris was such a good friend that he did not fire me for what I was doing, but I could tell his patience was slowly wearing thin with me.

Doug did the best he could during the holidays. Thanksgiving and Christmas were always tough on us to try to celebrate without my mother around because she loved that time of year so much. He would always make an awesome Thanksgiving dinner and Christmas dinner, but most of the time, I would eat and end up leaving because I needed a drink. For years, I spent my holidays intoxicated, trying to make myself feel good but with no success. I remember one year I woke up around noon and had no clue that it was even Christmas Day until I came out and saw Doug waiting for me so we could open presents. He did everything in his power to see that I had a happy holiday, and I did everything in my power to ruin them.

The following year Chris ended up closing the company down and going back to college for himself, so after three years of working together, I was now jobless with no plan of what to do with my life. Therefore, after working with Chris for those three years and parting ways, I found myself back in a deep depression. Most of my friends were well out of college, starting their careers, and I was now unemployed with nothing in sight as to what I was going to do. I remember being really resentful toward anyone who was doing well with his/her life, and I would always have a feeling of pity for myself. Seeing all my friends with their families healthy and happy and starting their new jobs really depressed me, and I was jealous that my life turned out the way that it did. Feeling sorry for myself only lasted when I was sober, then when I started drinking, the pity I felt turned into anger. I was angry that my mother was gone, angry that my life was going nowhere, and angry that everyone else was happy and I was always depressed. I was just angry at life itself.

Being as our house was so small, Doug really endured a lot living with me throughout those years. Watching me come home late at night with a group full of drunken people making noise at all hours of the night was his reality. He would often have talks with me the next day and tell me what I did the night before, but I would just laugh it off. The patience he kept with me was amazing to say the least.

One morning I walked into the house after being up all night and noticed that he was already up reading his Bible in the living room. He stopped me as I stumbled toward my room and said that he wanted to read some scripture with me in hopes that it would stick in my head and I would stop living the way I was. I sat with him and heard what he was reading to me, but I was not ready to fully give up my lifestyle. So it pretty much went in one ear and out the other.

I remember that morning so well, and it stuck in my head because of something Doug said to me after reading out of his Bible. After he had told me that I needed to come to God and turn my life around, I remember saying to him, "Well, I'm a good person. I just have a messed up life, but I believe in Jesus! I'm still going to heaven, right?"

He looked at me and did not answer. Then he said something that would always stick with me. He said, "I honestly don't know, Chris. Only God knows." Now up until that moment in my life, I was under the assumption that because I knew of Jesus, I was going to heaven, no matter how messed up my life was. I almost felt as if I was entitled to get to heaven due to all the terrible things I had to go through on earth. So when he didn't come back with "yeah, you're definitely going to heaven, Chris," my mind opened up a little bit, and I began to question what getting to heaven was really about. I know I had promised my mother I was going to see her again when my life was over, and I had to make sure that whatever it took to get to heaven, I was going to do it.

The years continued to pass by, and I bounced around from job to job, living paycheck to paycheck. I was now in my midtwenties and was no better off with my life than I was back when my mother had first died. I had worked anywhere I could find a steady job but never really lasted because of my drinking problems and being unreliable.

I had made a couple of semiattempts at getting sober, but they would only last a couple days. I would be right back to calling up someone to share a couple of drinks with. I was spending my time in the bars, partying and blowing all my money on the tabs that I would rack up throughout the week.

My main group of good friends that I spent all high school with all had full-time jobs, and I had lost touch with pretty much all of them. I had a group of new friends, but it really changed frequently to whoever was available for the night and wanted to drink with me. Throughout the years, I always had plenty of girlfriends and seemed to be the life of the party, but none of the relationships ever lasted because of my hectic lifestyle back then. Doug would keep trying to get me to stop and to give my life to Jesus, but I was so stubborn and addicted to the alcohol that I would ignore everything he had to say. But it never stopped him from trying.

My life was a disaster to say the least, and it was getting worse by the day. I would wake up hungover and take my daily walk down the hallway into the living room to see Doug watching this preacher on television talk about Jesus and walk right by it to the kitchen. At this point, I was not even drinking anymore to cover up the pain of my mother's death and everything else that I had buried inside of me. I was just drinking because I did not know how it felt to be sober anymore. The drinking and drugs that I had been using for the last five years had taken its toll already on my body, and I was really starting to feel it. The normal hangovers, instead of lasting a couple hours, now lasted the whole day, and the only way I could escape their discomfort was to use more. I had been trapped in a vicious cycle for years, and my body was slowly shutting down because of it.

One day Doug came home and told me he had something for me. I walked over to see what it was, and he handed me a Bible. He said that inside of this book were the answers to all my problems. I looked at it and said thanks, but I really had zero intentions of even opening it up. I remember taking it and putting it in a drawer in case any of my friends came over that night so they would not see it and make fun of me. Every time I would open that drawer, I would see that Bible, and every time I shut it, something inside of me told me that I needed to stop running from reading it. It was a strong feeling, unlike anything I had ever felt in my life, and trying to overpower it began to get tougher and tougher each time I opened the drawer and saw it.

A couple of months down the road, I ended up losing another job I had and was down on myself again. I had been up for a couple of days drinking and partying, and I was literally at the lowest point in my life that I had ever been. After years of run-ins with the law, fights, and drugs I was sitting in my room with the darkest type of depression I had ever dealt with in my entire life.

I thought back to all the years as a kid—how I was in such a rush to grow up and go to college and make something of myself. My mother and Doug instilled in my brain that I could be whatever I wanted to be in life, but what I had become was a living nightmare. I overheard in the living room Doug listening to the same preacher that he normally listened to every day, and the message that he was talking about hit me like a ton of bricks. He was reading out of the Bible in the book of Matthew chapter 11 verse 28 when Jesus said, "Come to me, all you who are weary and burdened, and I will give you rest." Now I was in disbelief that what the man was talking about had fit into my life almost perfectly. I could not believe what I was hearing; it was almost as if he was talking directly to me when I heard the man preach. I took it as a sign from God telling me that I did not need to run anymore from my problems; Jesus was going to take it from here.

I sat on my bed listening from the other room to what the preacher was saying on Doug's television. My heart was pounding because I knew this was not just a coincidence. God was trying to tell me something! The preacher continued to talk about breaking bondages of drugs and alcohol, and that the only way to get victory over these things is through the blood of Jesus Christ. As he was preaching, I walked over to my dresser and opened up the drawer where the Bible was, and I took it out for the first time. I knelt down on the floor of my room, holding the Bible, and I said, "Lord, please help me. I want out of this life, and I am so scared because I do not know how to stop. I've been running for so long, and I'm exhausted. Can you please help me?"

I poured my heart out that day because I knew that if I did not, I was not going to make it much longer living the way I was.

As I opened the Bible to try to follow what the preacher was reading from, I stumbled upon Matthew chapter 7 verse 7, which said, "Ask and it shall be given to you; seek and you will find; knock and the door will be opened to you." The words were literally jumping off the page at me as I stood there holding the Bible. At that moment, I started to repent for all the terrible things I had done and how I was living, and I asked God to forgive me. I remember feeling such a sense of peace that I had not felt in such a long time immediately afterward. I then made a promise to God that if He could get me a good job and bring into my life a wife and child to start my own family that I would never go back to that way of living again and I would give him all the praise and glory for helping me.

After I was done praying, I walked outside and just sat on my front porch steps, watching the neighborhood kids play in the street. It felt as if a huge burden that I had been carrying for years had finally been removed from me. Doug opened the door and came outside as I was sitting there and sat next to me on the steps. I put my arm around him as we sat there watching the kids play in the street together, reminiscing about Mom. She used to love to be outside with me and all my friends, playing ball on a hot summer day. I could picture her running around smiling but would always have to take a break because she would get tired trying to keep up with us kids. We sat there for a little while talking, but I never told Doug what just happened to me in my room that day.

After a couple minutes Doug got up to walk back inside, but before he did, he turned around and said to me, "Don't worry, where Mom is at now, she'll never have to worry about ever getting tired again, pal." I realized the same way God had given her rest from everything she was going through in life, He was now going to start with me in mine.

Chapter 15

Born Again

As I sit here today and write this book, a lot has changed in my life. It has been seven years since that lonely day I spent in my room, crying out to Jesus for help. I am now thirty-four years old, married to the most amazing woman. We have a beautiful three-year-old son, whom we love and adore, named Christopher. I have a terrific job, which I have been working at now for over six years, and my wife and I recently just purchased a house together. On top of everything else, I am proud to say that I have been clean and found victory over drugs and alcohol through my faith in Jesus Christ. I am literally living proof that if you call on God in the name of Jesus Christ, He will answer your prayers. Not just answer your prayers but also He will give you more than what you ask for in every capacity. God is not limited in any way.

I made a promise with the Lord that day that if He rewarded me a good job, a wife, and a child to start a family with, I would never go back to my old ways of living and that I would give Him all the praise and glory for it. Well, let's just say God has more than kept up his part of my petition, and this book is my way to tell others that God answers prayer.

Through the years, I dealt with friends around me who laughed and ridiculed me for believing in Jesus and trusting Him to save my life. Sad to say, some of the people that I used to hang out and party with are not alive any longer. Had I continued to live the way I used to, I now know that I may have suffered the same fate as they ultimately did. I have to recognize that it was not me but God who saved me from a life dominated by sin. My story is no different from the millions of people who, at that time in my life, had little if any relationship with Jesus Christ. There will only be a different outcome if anyone who desires a change in his/her life will call upon the name of Jesus Christ and repent of his/her sins. As I look back now, I realize that not only was my life saved when

I asked Jesus Christ into my heart but my soul and spirit were instantly changed from a life dominated by the sin nature, and now I live by the divine nature. No, I am not referring to having sinless perfection for the Bible does not teach such. What the Bible does teach is that the sin nature is not to have dominion over the believer. Romans 6:14 says, "For sin shall not have dominion over you, for you are not under the law but under grace."

In the beginning of the book, I told you that this book was going to help and save your soul. The Bible is all truth and must be read and understood. Only God can do this by His Word. This book will prayerfully point you in the proper direction. It is extremely important for you to understand that not only did I regain my physical life back but now my name has also been written in the Book of Life, and there I am guaranteed my place in heaven.

Once I decided to repent from my sins and asked to be washed clean with the blood of Jesus Christ, I was immediately saved. All the things I did and ways I used to live were nailed to His cross, and I'm totally and completely forgiven. Spiritually speaking, I was buried with Christ, raised with Christ, and now I live with Christ, a brand-new born-again believer. It says in 2 Corinthians 5:17,

"Therefore if any man be in Christ, he is a new creature [creation]. Old things are passed away, behold, all things are become new." However, none of this could have been possible without my sins being removed and my faith in Jesus Christ as my Savior being renewed.

Knowing who Jesus is does not guarantee that you are going to heaven. Because you wear a cross around your neck or a tattoo of Jesus does not guarantee nor merit your eternal salvation. Going to church, feeding the poor, making charity donations—none of these things alone will save your soul. Although these works are good in their right, they will not give us victory over sin. Our actions, whether pleasing to God or not, cannot remove our sins for us. In Ephesians 2:8–9 it says, "For by grace are ye saved through faith; and that not of yourselves: it is the gift of God: Not of works, lest any man should boast."

Our simple faith in Christ for what He did on the cross is the only sacrifice God will recognize to be saved. God cannot accept anything we *do* as humans to sanctify ourselves. The sin debt can only be satisfied by the perfect, spotless, Lamb of God (Jesus Christ and Him crucified). Our good works do not merit any salvation. If we could save ourselves from our sins by our efforts, then Jesus Christ would not have had to die for us.

The good news is that if you are reading this, it's not too late, and you still have time to repent and give your life to the Lord. The bad news is that many of you will procrastinate and think that you still have plenty of time to come to God. I used to think that life was all about having fun, and once I was older, I would eventually settle down and come to God like most old people did. Sad to say, many of the people I was partying with back then probably had the same mind-set, and unfortunately, some of them never made it to getting old.

Our lives here on earth are meaningless if we do not make a decision and make heaven our home. The Bible says in the book of Matthew 16:26, "For what is a man profited, if he shall gain the whole world, and lose his own soul?" Our souls are eternal, and based on what we do during this short time here on earth will determine where we will spend eternity. Either you will come to Jesus and receive everlasting life in heaven or you will be cast away with Satan in the burning pit of hell.

So heaven or hell, these are the two possible outcomes that every single one of us will face one day. The Bible describes heaven in 1 Corinthians 2:9, "What no eye has seen, nor ear heard, nor the heart of man imagined, what God has prepared for those who love him." Nothing I can write down right now can even remotely come close to how great God's kingdom will be. Our human minds are incapable of understanding how awesome heaven is and what God has planned for us.

On top of the simply amazing visual aspects of being there, we will never again have to suffer through each and every day the things that we as humans go through in our lives today. The Bible says in Revelation 21:4, "And God shall wipe away all tears from their eyes, and death shall be no more death, neither shall there be mourning, neither shall there be any more pain: for the former things are passed away." This is where you want to be, people, not the alternative option.

The other option that we can choose to go to when this life is over is a place called hell. You may have heard about hell in a movie or television show and have convinced yourself that it's not real and that it's just a made-up place designed to scare people to do good in life.

Well, I'm sorry to say, but hell is real. And it's the last place you ever want to be. The descriptions of hell in any Hollywood movie do not even scratch the surface of how terrible this place is. The Bible says in Revelation 14:11, "And the smoke of their torment ascendeth up forever and ever, and they have no rest, day or night." You will literally be in the worst pain you can think of, burning in fire every second of every day for eternity.

That last quote from the Bible alone should be reason enough for you to come to Jesus immediately to escape this horrible place. Matthew 13:50 says, "And shall cast them [the wicked] into the fiery furnace of fire: there shall be wailing and gnashing of teeth." You will be surrounded by other lost souls crying and grinding their teeth in agony forever and ever. This will be where you spend eternity if you do not come to Jesus Christ and repent of your sins, asking for forgiveness. The choice is yours, but I urge you all, do not procrastinate. You need to make the decision *now*.

Many people believe that because they have done so much wrong in life, God could not possibly forgive their sins. I am here to assure you that the Bible says no matter what you have done in your life, the Lord can take away all your sins in the blink of an eye and make you a born-again child of God. Not only can He take them away but He *wants* to take them away. He wants you to come to Him and allow the Holy Spirit to work in your life. It's not God who sends anyone to hell. In fact, they are sending themselves there by denying Him during their life. I beg of you to come to Jesus right now and make sure that your name is written down in the Lamb's Book of Life before it is too late. We are living in some terrible times on earth right now, and every second that goes by that you are not saved, you are risking your eternal salvation and the loss of your soul.

Time is of the essence for you to come to Jesus and allow Him to take control of your life. By reciting the simple prayer that I have added below, believing with all your heart and soul that Jesus is the Son of God and trusting in what He has done at the cross for our salvation, you will then be saved. It's important that when we pray, we are praying the right way as well. Praying to Mary, other saints, the pope, or anyone else other than God the Father in the name of Jesus Christ is wrong. Our prayers are to be directed to God in the name of Jesus alone, and then we are given direct access to God, who hears our every need when we commune with Him. Praying should also be a private event that you do alone in a quiet location with no interruptions between you and God. Here is the sinner's prayer:

> *Heavenly Father,*
>
> *I come to you in prayer asking for the forgiveness of my sins. I confess with my mouth and believe with my heart that Jesus is your Son and that He died on the cross at Calvary that I might be forgiven and have eternal life in the kingdom of heaven. Father, I believe that Jesus rose from the dead, and I ask you right now to come in to my life and be my personal Lord and Savior. I repent of my sins and will worship you all the days of my life. Because your word is truth, I confess with my mouth that I am born again and cleansed by the blood of Jesus!*
>
> *In Jesus's name, amen!*

Now that you have said this prayer, you are washed clean with the blood of Jesus Christ your Savior.

Congratulations, you have found the answer. You have found Jesus Christ, and you are born again. A new name has been added to the Lamb's Book of Life, and you are indeed saved, guaranteeing you eternal peace in the kingdom of heaven.

Being saved does not mean you will never again experience any problems in your life and that every day will be easy for you, which is not the case at all. In fact, the devil will now try to tempt you more than ever and do everything in his power to see you lose your faith, which, if allowed, will take away your salvation. It is up to us as believers to trust in Christ always but, when the devil tries to come against us and when we sin, remember to come back to the cross and repent. "Ask and it shall be given."

We serve such a loving and patient God, but unless we seek and ask for it, grace isn't given to us automatically. It is your job now to go out into the world and spread the good news of Jesus Christ and do your best to witness to your unsaved family and friends. Remind them of the need to accept Christ as their personal Savior. Matthew 28:18–20 says, "And Jesus came and spoke unto them saying, All power is given unto me in Heaven and in

Earth. Go ye therefore and teach all nations, baptizing them in the name of the Father, and of the Son, and of the Holy Spirit. Teaching them to observe all things whatsoever I have commanded you; and, lo I am with you always, even to the end of the world."

Chapter 16

Closing Thoughts

God has a specific plan for each and every one of us, whether we know it or not. I spent years wondering as to why I had to endure losing everyone that I loved in life. I never blamed God, but I was confused as to why nobody around me had gone through any of the pain that I had consistently gone through. However, as I look back now, it is so clear to me. Remember in the beginning of the book when I quoted Torrance Nash saying, "The greater the calling, the greater the test"? God will allow things to happen in our life in order to see how we will react and how strong our faith is. I believe He is now 100 percent using me to spread His Word and to help others due to my faithfulness toward Him through my trials in life. I give Him all the praise and glory for selecting me, and I will always be obedient to His calling.

As I sit back and look at some old pictures of my family and me when I was growing up, I realize how important a role each and every one of them has played in my journey in life. I am so very grateful to have had the mother I had, who loved me unconditionally, but more importantly, who always taught me how important it was for me to find Jesus in life and to trust in Him through it all. From the moment before I was born when she prayed for a child to her very last second on earth when she prayed to God in the hospital before she died, she always kept her faith in Jesus.

I used to get upset when I would think about my mother and how she died, but now I look at pictures of her and I smile because I know that we will again be together in heaven with the Lord. I have not seen my mother's face in over thirteen years now, and not a day goes by that I don't think about her, missing her warm smile. We had twenty-one years together here on earth, and we will have eternity to catch up with each other when it's my time to go and meet the Lord. I will see you when I get there, Mom, love you.

My biological dad played an important part in my journey as well, whether he realized it or not. Everything that had transpired while he was alive, when I was a child, was all done for a reason. Though at the time I was confused and disturbed at what had taken place, I can look back now and realize it was all part of God's plan. Only God knows whether or not my real dad made it to heaven. I pray that he called out to the Lord before he died and asked God for forgiveness. If he had, then I will also see him again one day in the kingdom of heaven. My dad lived a tough life, but no matter how tough life had gotten, had he just turned to Jesus in his time of struggle, he would have found relief. And he probably would still be here today. I look at his pictures also and I smile knowing that he loved me. I just pray that he looked for Jesus before leaving this earth.

I want to take this time to thank my wife, Jess, and son, Christopher. I was in a rough place before either of you came into my life, but I just want you to know how much you both truly mean to me. I sat down and prayed about you both before I even knew who you both would be, and the Lord answered my prayers.

Jess, we have been together going on seven years now, and I can honestly say you are my best friend and one true love of my life. The greatest thing we both share in life is that we both have the same mutual love for Jesus. It is a wonderful thing to live in a home like the one I had growing up with two parents teaching their child the importance of God in their lives. I thank God every day that he brought us together and pray that He continues to bless us in every way.

To my son, Christopher, your daddy loves you more than you will ever know. I need you to know, son, that no matter where you end up in life, just always remember to trust in Jesus and that He is there for you. He should be the center of all the things you do, and if this life ever gets you down, you can always rely on Him for the answers.

I love you both so much. You truly are gifts from above and not a second goes by that I do not thank God for answering my prayers when I asked for you both.

Last, but certainly not the least, I thank my father, Doug. As I stated in chapter 1, you have been the most influential person in my entire life. I cannot thank you enough for all that you have done for me through the years and continue to do for me to this day. I truly believe

God puts people in your life for certain reasons, and as I look back now, it's so clear as to why he used you in my life. You have been the best father, friend, and role model that I could have asked for.

Looking back at all the memories I have as a kid of you helping me with my fastball, learning to ride a bike, and being there with me through high school and college, I realize that the most important thing that you did for me was lead me to Jesus. All those years I was lost, you never gave up on me once. You would just sit me down every single time and let me know that all I needed was Jesus. Jesus, Jesus, Jesus—not rehab, not a therapist. All I need is Jesus in my life to overcome all my problems. I thank the Lord every day for allowing you into my life, and I honestly do not know where I would be today without you. From the bottom of my heart, I want to say thank you and that I love you, pal.

Therefore, to conclude this book, I think it is important to acknowledge the fact that this is not how the story ends. The fight continues every day for us who believe, and it is up to us now to spread the word to others. Just as my mother and Doug have taught me the importance of having God in my life, we will continue to do the same for our son, and I urge you to do the same. Satan wants you to lose your soul and turn your back on God. The devil is the one who is behind your addictions and problems in your life. God is the answer to them. I pray that you find your way to the Lord and accept Jesus as your personal Lord and Savior. It is the most important thing you will ever do in your entire life. The gift of a new life and eternal salvation in the kingdom of heaven is right in front of you. All you have to do is ask, and *it shall be given*.

Printed in the United States
By Bookmasters